Modern Museum Management

Cataloging in Publication Data — DK
[Courtesy: D.K. Agencies (P) Ltd. <docinfo@dkagencies.com>]

Gupta, S.P. (Swarajya Prakash), 1931–2007.
Modern museum management / S.P Gupta, Mohit Srivastava.
p. cm.
With special reference to India.
Includes bibliographical references (p.)
ISBN 13: 9788124604458 ISBN 10: 8124604452

1. Museums — Management. 2. Museums — India — Management. 3. Museums — Collection management. 4. Museum — Collection management — India. 5. Art objects — Conservation and restoration. 6. Art objects — Conservation and restoration — India. I. Srivastava, Mohit, 1978- , joint author. II. Title.

DDC 069.068 22

ISBN 13: 978-81-246-0445-8 (Pbk) ISBN 10: 81-246-0445-2
First published in India, 2010

Published by:
Indraprastha Museum of Art and Archaeology
B-17, Qutab Institutional Area, New Delhi - 16
and
D.K. Printworld (P) Ltd.
Regd. Office: 'Srikunj', F-52, Bali Nagar
Ramesh Nagar Metro Station, New Delhi – 15
Phones: (011) 2545 3975; 2546 6019 *Fax*: (011) 2546 5926
E-mail: indology@dkprintworld.com
Website: www.dkprintworld.com

Printed by: D.K. Printworld (P) Ltd., New Delhi.

Preface

"MUSEUM is for the people, with the people, and of the people" is the basic theme on which the book is written. The book critically examines the museums and the extent to which they are fulfilling the expectations of the people, and provides a useful guideline for their improvements.

This book was the dream of Late Dr S.P. Gupta which he could not fulfill during his life. Today is a great day. The book is finally being printed and he would definitely be very happy in heaven.

This work covers all aspects of managing a museum — establishment, administration, acquisition of objects, security, marketing, conservation methods etc. — in short, this will serve as a comprehensive guide book for students of museology and for those in the museum profession.

I would like to thank my great teachers Late Dr G.N. Pant, Dr A.K. Das, Dr Satya Vrat Tripathi and Shri M.C. Gupta for their support and guidance from time to time.

I express my sincere gratitude to Shri K.N. Dikshit, Shri O.P. Tandon and Shri S.S. Biswas of Indian Archaeological Society for their valuable suggestions. I am also thankful to my colleagues Shri Kulbhushan Mishra and Shri Bharat Singh for their support and encouragement.

Thanks are also due to Shri Susheel Mittal of D.K. Printworld (P) Ltd. and his staff for their hard work during the publication of this book and for bringing out this book in an attractive manner.

Mohit Srivastava

Contents

1

Museum

Origin, Definition, Scope, Types and Development

Origin

"MUSEUM," *sangrahalaya* in Hindi, is the most commonly used term for a place where objects of interest of common man as well as of scholars are housed and at least some of which are displayed for people to see. There is hardly any country in the world in which there is no museum.

The word "museum" has been adopted in English from Latin. But the Latin language itself derived it from the Greek word "museion," which stands for a "temple dedicated to the muses." But who are the muses? "Muses" are the Greek goddesses of arts and sciences, i.e. various kinds of artistic and scientific knowledge. These are broadly like the Indian goddess Sarasvati. In the beginning, there were only three "muses" which eventually grew to nine, from the period of Hesiod onwards. In Greek mythology, all these nine muses are the unmarried daughters of father Zeus, the king of gods, and mother Mnemasyne, "the goddess of memory." These were born at the foothills of Mount Olympus in Greece. Each one of these goddesses, it is believed, presides over a particular branch of art, science and literature. Thus,

Calliope is the goddess of poetry, Euterpe of lyrics, Thalia of comedy, Melphomene of tragedy, Trspischore of dance, Erato of love (same as Eros out of which the term "erotic" emerged), Polyhymnic of religious hymns, Urania of astronomy, and Clio of history. The subject of museology is, however, not confined to the Greek term of "muses," meaning entertainment. It has now developed into a systematic discipline with its specific philosophy and ethics, use of scientific methodologies and instruments in preserving and conserving the works of art, and ways and methods to display the exhibits so that they are preserved for the future generations, without getting damaged further, and eventually become a source of knowledge to the visitors.

The oldest museum in the world, as the records show, was established at Alexandria on the mouth of the river Nile in Egypt, overlooking the sea. The city of Alexandria was founded in fourth century BCE by Alexander the Great as the name itself suggests. Ptolemy I (Soter) of Egypt (325–285 BCE), the successor of Alexander, enriched the city with art objects as well as objects of curiosity and rare manuscripts. The library of Alexandria had four lakh manuscripts in the form of tablets of baked clay engraved with inscriptions written in cuneiform script. As time passed, this library-cum-museum became a great centre of learning where scholars from countries located far and wide came to enhance their knowledge. It is a pity that the Islamic Arabs, when they invaded Egypt in the seventh century CE, also plundered and destroyed this great repository of the sources of ancient wisdom. Thus, the greatest museum, library, archives, university, research centre, all in one, was lost to humanity for all time to come by Islamic vandalism. Nevertheless, there is no denying the fact that the format and functioning of this very museum gave birth to the idea and concept of "museums" which has been adopted by people universally.

Definition

People have been giving various definitions to the term "museum," but we will discuss here only two of them, the ICOM's (International Council of Museums) definition and the Museums Association of the United Kingdom's definition. The ICOM gives the following definition.

> A museum is a non-profit making, permanent institution in the service of society and of its development, and open to the public, which acquires, conserves, researches, communicates and exhibits, for purposes of study, education and enjoyment, material evidence of people and their environment.

The Museums Association (United Kingdom), however, gives its own definition:

> A museum is an institution which collects, documents, preserves, exhibits and interprets material evidence and associated information for the public benefit.

As may be seen from the above, there is hardly any fundamental difference between the two definitions; the difference is only in phraseology since both of them give emphasis on collection-making, preserving the collected material, displaying it for the public as well as making the collection available to the researchers.

Museology

The term "museology" has a history of only half a century or so. It developed after the Second World War. The Museums Division of the UNESCO at Paris had developed it since it was realized that unless we develop the concept of "museum" in a theoretical formulation and design systematically knowledge-based approach to the subject, museums even in the twenty-first century, will remain at the old level of *ajaibghar* or "the house of curious" or fantastic things; they will neither be a place of learning or "centre of teaching and public education" as they are these days. Thus, by adding the epithet "logy," the subject of museology becomes a scientific subject with systematic approach to every activity done in the museum, from collecting and packaging an object to its display in showcases in the museum.

Its role in society is also fully defined. Specific systems for research, conservation and education have been worked out. The classification of different kinds of museums has also been worked out and systematized. Museology is, therefore, taken to be "the branch of knowledge concerned with the study of the purpose and organization of museums."

Scope

The ultimate aim of the modern museum is "the welfare of the society by creating a knowledge-based human-resource." Museums are, therefore, accountable to public at large, also because it utilises public money and even taxes collected by the governments which support many of them. Thus, it is the responsibility of the museum to serve the society. This it does by collecting, documenting, preserving and exhibiting objects as well as disseminating the knowledge about its collection by making research-based as well as popular publications on them either through print-media or electronic-media, or both.

The primary or the first stage work of the museum is the collection of objects the nature of which depends on the specific subject or subjects for which it is established. Photo-documentation of these objects follows since it is necessary for not only record and security purposes but also for several other purposes. For example, it provides legal ownership of the objects to the museum. In case of theft, the stolen object may be traced from any part of the world, including another museum if it has been sold there. The new owner as well as the thief may then be liable for punishment under several international laws. He or she will also have to return it to the owner-museum. If secretly sold to some museum, that museum will have to return it to the parent museum, according to international conventions and laws now in force.

Preserving and proper upkeep of heritage and handing over them to the next generation is the basic duty of the museums devoted to the collection of objects of heritage both tangible, i.e. material items, such as the works of art and craft, and intangible, i.e. non-material items, such as the music, dance, drama, oral and folk literature, etc.

Exhibition is all about display of museum objects in a proper way for which norms have been laid. It should be attractive, properly lighted, and clearly visible from all the angles, be placed on the eye-level and accompanied by proper labels describing basic data about the object.

Nowadays education is one of the most important works that a modern museum is expected to perform. Education is a comprehensive term. It includes arranging popular lectures on museum-collection, special lectures by specialists and scholars, and also includes harnessing the services of those teachers who are trained to interact with illiterate as well as under-privileged, physically and mentally challenged and visually-impaired people and impart knowledge.

Types

The subject of museology now accepts the principle that "there may be as many kinds of museums as there are kinds of objects, both man-made and natural." Every subject and every object of this universe comes in the range of museums. That is why we now see the museums existing in the world on a wide variety of subjects listed below and many others not listed here — Art Museum, Archaeology Museum, Site Museum, Science Museum, Health Museum, Agriculture Museum, Police Museum, Shoes Museum, Toilet Museum, Philatelic Museum, Archives, Dolls Museum, Children Museum, Rail Museum, Textile Museum, Utensil Museum, Industrial Museum, Forest Museum, Sports Museum, Natural History Museum, Personalia Museum, War Museum, Air Force Museum, Crafts Museum, Sanskriti Museum, Geological Museum, Anthropological Museum, Tribal Museum, Museum of Man, Museum of Musical Instruments, etc. The range is really open-ended. As a matter of fact some authorities include even cognate institutions of Aquarium, Planetarium, Botanical gardens, Zoological garden.

Development

It is often held that the first modern museum of the world was Ashmolean Museum which was set up in the Oxford University in the year 1683, i.e. about 350 years ago. It was aimed at preserving the collection of one Mr Tradescant, a Dutchman who had donated it to the university to preserve it in a museum. The list of ten old museums of the world is as follows:

1. Ashmolean Museum, Oxford University, England — CE 1683
2. British Museum, London, England — CE 1753
3. Charleston Museum, Philadelphia, U.S.A. — CE 1773
4. Belvedere Museum, Austria — CE 1781
5. The Louvre Museum, Paris, France — CE 1793
6. The National Gallery of Art, Haarlem, Holland — CE 1800
7. National Museum, Budapest, Hungary — CE 1802
8. Pennsylvania Academy of Fine Arts, U.S.A. — CE 1805
9. National Museum, Copenhagen, Denmark — CE 1807
10. Indian Museum, Calcutta, India — CE 1814

In the Indian context the concept of museum is, however, very old. There are innumerable references in Sanskrit literature dating back to at least the Gupta period of the fifth century CE which suggest that in one form or the other paintings and other kinds of works of art were "collectively put on display," which is how a modern museum is defined. There are three such terms: *chitra-shala, chitra-vithi,* and *ranga-mahal* in the ancient Indian literature. The *chitrashala* exhibited paintings and sculptures as well as other objects of decorative arts since the term *chitra* means "works of visual art." These were the art galleries usually established in the palaces of kings and nobles. We also find *chitrashala* in temples and other kinds of community-centres. Here too objects of visual art were put on display for the general visitors and pilgrims. Such exhibits included paintings, etc. done on religious themes, generally mythological themes, obviously to educate the visiting faithful in their own religions. We find, on the other hand, decorative and colourful wall-paintings in *ranga-mahal* which were especially created for the kings and the members of their families. They usually contained family portraits. The *chitravithi,* on the other hand, represents the place where paintings, etc. were put on exhibition; *vithi* means a long hall or gallery. *Vithi,* therefore, signifies such a place which is spacious but more in length than breadth. However, later on this "narrowness" of the space sense was overlooked. Now any room or hall or corridor where works of art and crafts are put on exhibition is called "gallery" or "art gallery." There is, however, a slight difference between a "gallery" and a "museum." The difference lies mainly in scope. While a gallery is generally devoted to a single theme, such as paintings, manuscripts or arms, a museum may be devoted to multiple themes — art, archaeology, anthropology, etc. like the National Museum, New Delhi.

The modern-day museum concept, however, entered India with the birth of the Asiatic Society of Bengal. This Society was founded by Sir William Jones in 1784 in Kolkata. It was soon turned into the Oriental Museum of the Asiatic Society in Kolkata in the year 1814. The "Oriental Museum" was, however, re-named as "Indian Museum" as late as 1866, through an Act of Parliament, called "Indian Museum Act." It had, of course, shifted to the present building, a little later, in 1875, and was opened to the public on 1 April 1875. This was the first public museum in India established with government support.

Museum movement in India got a boost with the birth of Archaeological Survey of India (abbreviated hereafter as ASI) in 1861, the year in which Sir Alexander Cunningham became the first Director General of ASI. Since then ASI has been exploring and excavating archaeological sites and enriching museums with antiquarian remains. A chain of what are called "site-museums," i.e. the museums established at the archaeologically excavated or explored site, were established by the ASI. The first site-museum established by the ASI was at Sarnath, in 1910. It was followed by many other similar museums, established at Mathura, Sanchi, Pataliputra (Patna), Khajuraho, Amaravati, Lothal, etc.

When Sir Mortimer Wheeler became the Director General of ASI, in 1944, a "Museums Branch" was set up in ASI to maintain these museums. The condition of museums has now greatly improved. Presently, there are more than 40 site museums of ASI being looked after by their circle officers who are, however, meant primarily to conserve monuments under their charge since the Museums Branch was abolished by a short-sighted IAS officer who became DG, ASI.

The case of Central Asian Antiquities Museum, New Delhi was slightly different. It was set up in 1929 in ASI to house the collection of around 11,000 art and archaeological objects collected by Sir Aurel Steim between 1901 and 1916, during three of his major expeditions conducted in Chinese Central Asian Republic of Xin-xiang or Sinkiang. It is now shifted to the National Museum, New Delhi.

The Mathura Museum was founded by the then collector of the district Mathura, Mr F.S. Growse, in the year 1874. The collections were shifted to the present building in the year 1930. It has the world's best sculptures of Mathura art, mainly Kushana and Gupta, and largely Buddhist.

Markham (Secretary, British Museums Association) and Hargreaves (DG, ASI) submitted a report in 1936 with a chapter on museums. It surveyed as many as 105 museums at that point of time. The report suggested to the Government of India to take steps to improve their functioning. There were a few more similar reports instituted by the Government of India from time to time dealing with the same subject.

The story of the birth of the National Museum, New Delhi began with an Exhibition of Indian Art, consisting of selected sculptures from various museums of India, sponsored by the Royal Academy, London, with the cooperation of the Governments of India and Britain. It was on display in the galleries of Burlington House, London during the winter months of 1947-48. On its return to India, it was decided by Pt. Jawaharlal Nehru to display the same collection under a single roof in Delhi before the return of the exhibits to their respective museums in India. Accordingly, the exhibition was held in the State Rooms of the Rashtrapati Bhawan, New Delhi in 1949 which turned out to be a great success. In turn, the event eventually proved responsible for the creation of the National Museum at New Delhi. On the 15 August 1949, the National Museum was formally inaugurated by the then Governor-General of India, Shri C. Rajagopalachari, and it was announced that till a permanent building for housing the National Museum was constructed, the Museum would continue to function from the Rashtrapati Bhawan. In the meanwhile, the foundation of the present building was laid by Pt. Jawaharlal Nehru, the then Prime Minister of India, on 12 May 1955. The Museum was formally thrown open to the public in the present building on 18 December 1960. And it is now within the administrative control of the Department of Culture, Government of India.

Teaching of Museology in India

Teaching of museology also drew the attention of authorities in India. The Museology Course in India started from the

M.S. University, Baroda in 1952. The Institute of Archaeology of ASI started a Diploma Course in 1959; at that point of time it was called "School of Archaeology." Museology was one of the subjects taught in this course. It was later followed by the University of Calcutta, Banaras Hindu University, Aligarh Muslim University, Pilani Institute of Technology and Science, Bhopal University, National Museum Institute, New Delhi, etc.

It is hoped that the subject of museology will attract more and more young students and talented specialists.

2

Educational Role of Museums

"EDUCATION through Recreation" is the basic concept of a museum's role in a nation's education system which is based upon "class-room teaching." Thus, "museum" is nowadays considered an institution for imparting non-formal education. It cultivates first the general awareness about the heritage and then gives correct information about its collection to people. Museum provides visual interaction to visitors with the objects under its charge. In modern days, museums have provided adequate facility for academic and pedagogical researches as well. For the lay person, "visual experiences" and "interactive knowledge" are more important than formal academic approaches to learning.

There could be many ways to provide education to visitors in the museum. Well arranged guided-tours and gallery-talks are considered the best because of personal interaction of the visitor and the educator. However, carefully prepared museum literature, containing pamphlets, handouts, gallery-sheets, brochures, guide-books, picture postcards, catalogues, newsletter, research monographs, etc. are of permanent value for the visitors. Workshops, seminars and symposiums are arranged to promote research at higher level. A museum should have, as far as possible, an auditorium to be used variously for educational purposes. In it the authorities can arrange film shows related to the themes the museum is engaged in. Cultural programmes by performing artistes engaged in dance and drama can also be used to educate people in subjects we want them to know about. Debate and live demonstrations by the artistes can also form part of the same scheme of imparting non-formal education. A Reference Library with the books for various age groups is also now a must for a modern museum. The practice of opening a museum shop within the museum premises, where photographs, plaster-casts, video-cassettes, CD ROMs, souvenirs, models and reproductions can be purchased at a reasonable price, has become universal since it brings the same people again and again to a museum, which normally does not happen. It becomes very effective if a restaurant is also run for the visitors. Museum celebrations like Museum Day, Museum Week, Museum Fortnight, Cultural Events, Special/Temporary exhibitions are the opportunities by which a museum attracts people to visit it repeatedly and, thereby, get educated in a very subtle fashion.

Museum and School Education

The National Education Policy was passed by the Parliament in 1986. It strongly recommended students' visit to museums for education by seeing actual objects and knowing about them directly, which alone is the best way to learn. For primary school stage the policy says

> Setting up in schools of museum corners largely with collections made by students themselves in the form of stones, feathers, leaves, etc.

For Middle/High/Secondary schools, the policy says,

> Networking of various schools for visits to museums, libraries, galleries and monuments maintained by the State and the Central Archaeological Surveys. Setting up of museum corners with models, illustrations, posters, charts, books and with objects collected by students from their neighbourhood, including local crafts, flowers, leaves, feathers, etc.

For University level, the policy says,

> Earmarking of separate space in colleges for painting, gallery of art, facilities for photography, sculpture, etc. Networking with the schools in the neighbouring area for putting up of mobile exhibitions or conducted tours by school students to these special rooms/galleries put up for cultural displays.

These policy statements underline the fact that there is a lot of merit in museum education for students of all levels, from Primary to College.

Ideally, every museum should have an Education Department headed by an education specialist. Museum education specialist should be trained in the psychology of learning and may have considerable experience of analysing complex concepts and presenting them in a simple way to a non-specialist audience. Since art and science of communication is basic to this kind of endeavour, the museum educators must undergo courses offered by various organizations dealing with pedagogy.

Contact with Schools and Teachers Training Programmes

Museum Education Department has the responsibility to contact local school teachers and make sure that the schools know what is going on at the museum and how they can make use of its services. In 1932 Robert Franceller said that "museum educator" (Docent) is not adequate to guide school children; school children should be guided by their teachers because teachers know the learning capacity and requirements of children. So, if the school teachers will guide the school children then it will be necessary to train them, to tell them how to see museum objects in detail, their iconography, the usage, material, purpose, social relevance, casting technique, etc. Every museum, at least once a year, should organize teachers' training programme. The message is clear and loud. The emphasis is laid on the formal training of the museum educators, and untrained educators are discouraged.

Museum Visit

Every museum visit of school children must be planned carefully by teachers and museum staff of the Education Department. The museum visit should be a part of the curriculum and linked with the school education as has been suggested in the policy quoted above. The preparation for the museum visit, therefore, takes place in the classroom. An introduction of the museum and its activities are to be given in the classroom in advance, so that when children go to the museum they will already have a good idea of what things they are going to see and what work they are going to do by way of exercise or photography or making sketches of objects on display.

While arriving, school children deserve a warm, relaxed and friendly welcome by the museum staff. Thereafter, proper orientation about the museum, its galleries and precious works of art and crafts should be provided to them. Every museum should have the provision of Education Room or Discovery Room where lecture may be delivered followed by activity-oriented programmes, like workshops, quiz shows, puppet shows, film shows, dance, drama, debate, performances, painting competition, etc.

School Loan Services

The lending of museum objects to schools is commonly called school loan services. The principle behind it is that the real museum objects, of which there are several other examples in the museum collection, for example, copper coins of a particular variety of king Kanishka, or else replicas of sculptures, such as those of Buddha, are lent for short periods of time to schools, so that teachers can integrate learning from objects into their normal class work. Objects which might otherwise simply remain in store may also serve a real educational purpose in the hands of teachers and children. The objects are provided in specially-designed boxes accompanied by notes for teachers. An ideal loan-kit may contain museum objects or replicas, articles, charts, maps, slides, some worksheets, audio-video enhancements like cassettes, CD, DVD, and a suggestion book where teachers could write the effects of these things on children.

Sharing experience and feedback data is the key to develop new strategies for education.

Museum Corner

Museums should encourage schools to open at least one museum corner in their premises. A museum may provide consultancy, electricians, carpenters and other technical staff to schools and enrich their museum corner with plaster-casts, models, dioramas, photographs, etc. in what is called "Participatory Educational Strategy" which is now considered world over as the best way of learning since "doing is learning" is basic to all kinds of process of acquiring knowledge of the visual world.

3

Museum Management

For maintaining and managing museum properly, classification of its functions is necessary. We can classify museum functions into three main headings:

1. Collection
2. Documentation
3. Exhibition

Collection

It is rightly said that a museum may collect anything but cannot collect everything. Every museum should have, therefore, some "Collection Policy," written or unwritten, though preferably written. This "Policy Document," so to say, clearly defines the scope of a museum's collection. In other words, in this document it must be clearly mentioned as to what are the things the museum will collect. For example, a Rail Museum will collect only railway-related objects and not art and archaeological objects. Similarly, an Art and Archaeology museum will not collect contemporary objects related to physics or chemistry or astronomy, it will collect objects related to art and archaeology only.

There are so many methods by which a museum can acquire objects.

PURCHASE

Museum can enrich its collection by purchase. For this purpose a museum should normally have a committee of experts. This committee consists of experts in the related fields of study — coins, epigraphy, painting, bronze, manuscripts, etc. if it is a history or archaeology museum. The museum may appoint some outside experts also as members of this committee. The director of the museum normally works as its member-secretary. This committee is responsible for evaluating and pricing the artefacts. The museum concerned normally publishes advertisements in different newspapers about the categories of objects the museum will like to purchase in the open market from those who have such objects, with terms and conditions. It initially demands photographs with full details. The advertisement should mention the fact that "if approved by the expert committee" the person will be called to the museum on such and such date and time to present the object to the committee for examination and price-negotiation. First, the dealer tells his own price and then the committee fixes the price; if the dealer agrees then the deal is done, otherwise some bargaining is allowed in this process from both the sides. After the deal, a contract is signed by the dealer with the museum. According to this contract the museum will keep the object for a certain period of time, may be for three or five years and check its authenticity by various scientific methods and international authorities. If the object is found fake then it will be returned and the price-money will be taken back.

GIFT

This has proved to be the most favoured method of acquiring objects for museums. The museum may get prestigious and priceless objects by this method. For example Mrs and Mr Nasli Heeramaneck had once donated their pre-Columbian collection to the National Museum, New Delhi when they saw that it totally lacked in this regard. Ms Saran Rani Vaklival also donated her very significant musical instruments collection to the National Museum, New Delhi. Dr A.P. Khatri donated his entire prehistory and palaeontology collection to the Indraprastha Museum, New Delhi. Gift should be acknowledged by putting the name of the donor in the individual label.

ARCHAEOLOGICAL EXPEDITION

Artefacts explored, or unearthed in excavations at an archaeological site also enrich museums in terms of movable antiquities. Almost all the site museums are the by-products of such expeditions. Archaeological museums can send their own expeditions for this purpose. These scientific expeditions are also a very useful method for collecting authentic objects for ethnographical and anthropological museums.

TREASURE TROVE

According to Indian Treasure Trove Act, buried treasure belongs to the government in the sense that government has the right to acquire any work of art found even accidentally, say in one's cultivated field. It can keep full or parts of the treasure but it will have to pay compensation to the discoverer equal to one and a half times of the market price; the 50 per cent premium is offered as an inducement to the owner not to destroy or sell the treasure, or else melt it for the metal.

CONFISCATION

Articles confiscated by police, army, custom officers, income-tax authorities during raids, etc. also enrich museums. Sometimes, Courts of Law also pass orders to the museum to keep such articles under *superdari,* i.e. under custody of a certain museum till the case is decided finally.

BEQUEST

Some people give money to buy other man's collections, or their own collections after their death, through a Will, of course.

EXCHANGE

Exchange of artefacts between one museum (Indian or foreign) and the other provide diversity to the collection of the museum. Exchanges can be made on permanent basis or for a particular period of time through written contract.

LOAN

There are two kinds of loan — (i) temporary or short-term loan, and (ii) long-term, or else perpetual or permanent loan. Short-term loan is given generally by big museums to small museums for a specific period of time. The idea behind the short-term loan is that the objects which might otherwise simply remain in the Store will find a place in a gallery of another museum for people to see, enjoy and study. Long-term loan remains in the museum for long periods of time. For example, Archaeological Survey of India has given many archaeological artefacts from their excavations conducted at Harappa and Mohenjo-Daro on long-term loan to the National Museum, New Delhi.

Documentation

If galleries are the "face" of the museum, then documentation is certainly its "brain." It keeps not only the records of the museum objects, including the original information concerning them; it also controls their entry and exit.

IDENTIFICATION TAG

This is the first, what is called, "identification record" of the museum object. The following items are written on this tag which is tied with the object in question:

1. Name of the object
2. Name of the donor/dealer
3. Date and time of the entry in the museum for keeping in safe-custody
4. Donor's or seller's full address or addresses with phone nos., etc.
5. Measurements of objects with weight
6. Overall physical condition
7. Signature of the donor/dealer
8. Signature of the museum authority

TEMPORARY RECEIPT

This is an important and also confidential record. The following are the points written in this record:

1. Accession no. (Adhoc no. given by the museum)
2. Source (from whom or which agency the object has come)
3. Date of Entry in the museum
4. Short description of the object
5. Condition of preservation
6. Purpose for which received
7. Disposal (given back to owner/taken on long-term loan, etc.)

Adhoc no. is given to the object at the time of its arrival at the museum in case it has to remain there even overnight. The receipt bearing the above details also contains two conditions on the backside:

1. The museum will give the same treatment and affection as it gives to other objects in its own collection but in case of fire, flood, theft and other mishap the museum will not be responsible.
2. In case of death or non-availability of the primary owner, the authorization of the object is given to . . . (name, address, etc. of the nominee appointed by the primary owner which he is obliged to give as a part of the legal contract).

GENERAL ACCESSION REGISTER

General Accession Register (GAR) is the most important

document in a museum. It is the centralized register of the museum in which every object coming into the museum at any point of time through any means must be entered in the GAR. It is a semi-legal document of the museum. It is like the FIR of a case in the police station. It bears running sequential numbers with dates and is never changed. There can be two types of GAR in the museum:

1. Loose-leaf Register
2. Bound Register

The advantage of loose-leaf register is that we can go on adding or subtracting any page easily. It is thus very easy to handle. In it each page can be typed separately. If any mistake takes place due to any reason a new page can be added instead of the same old page. The disadvantage of this register is that anybody can damage or remove or play fraud with any page easily. Bound register, on the other hand, consists of a limited number of pages. In it each page is paginated (by machine) bearing a separate number. Nobody can add or subtract any page. We cannot type its pages. Every line of this register is handwritten. This register needs a lot of attention. No mistake should normally occur in this register. Microfilming and computer entry of its data is very much required. This is the most confidential record of the museum; so the museum curator should not show it to other persons as far as possible. In the beginning loose-leaf register was in practice in India. Markham and Hargreves also wrote in their report in 1936 that loose-leaf registers were common in practice in Indian museums at that time. But, now most of the museums are using bound registers. Bound register is also recommended for the museums by museologists even if the mistakes occur and cuttings are made, however, the cuttings must be countersigned by two authorised persons of the museum.

According to International Committee for Documentation (CIDOC), which is a very important body of International Council of Museums (ICOM), a GAR should contain the following information —

1. Museum number of the object (Acc. No.)
2. Name of the museum
3. Name of the administrative set-up (Dirctor/Curator/Keeper)
4. General classification (Painting/Bronze/etc.)
5. Location in the museum (Painting Section/Archaeology Deptt./etc.)
6. Geographical origin of the object (Bengal/Southern Gujarat/etc.)
7. Specific name of the object (Buddha head/Shivalinga/etc.)
8. Artist (craftsman) name/date of birth/signature (Raza, 1958, etc.)
9. Material (Paper/Stone/Canvas/Bronze, etc.)
10. Technique ("Lost-wax"/oil, etc.)
11. Acquisition — Date/Method/Place
12. Purchase/Price
13. Name of the person responsible for acquisition

14. Cultural group to which the object belongs (Mishin tribe in Majuli island, Assam/etc.)
15. Function of the object (for killing animal during sacrifice/etc.)
16. Date of the object (19th century/CE 514/etc.)
17. Style/School/Influence
18. Historical background of the object (Shivaji had used it for killing Afzal Khan/etc.)
19. Condition of Preservation
20. Old inventory no.
21. Reference in the catalogue (if published)

ACCESSION NUMBER

Each object in a museum is identified by its Accession Number. When an object comes to the museum it is given a permanent number called Accession No. Two objects in a museum cannot hold one and the same Accession no. These days three-tier numbering system (tripartite numbering system or decimal number system) is being commonly used in museums. The first part signifies "the year of accessioning" while the second part tells us "the serial number against which the object has been listed in that particular year," for example, 98.11 will denote that the object was accessioned in the GAR of the year 1998 against the serial no. 11. If the object has some movable item found detached then the third part will tell us the serial number of that particular object. For example, if a museum object holds no. 95.58.3 then it will mean that this object arrived in the museum in 1995, 58 is the serial no. of that particular year that means museum had already acquired 57 objects prior to this object. The no. 3 signifies that the object has at least 3 movable parts, this one is the third.

MARKING

For writing Accession Number on the object proper marking is absolutely necessary. Each object in a museum needs marking. Marks on the object should be permanent, clear, and readily accessible, but so placed that they will not detract from the appearance of the object. Marking materials vary somewhat according to the objects. In general, museums are using Indian black ink for pottery and sculptures; artists' oil colour for glass, metal, ceramics, wood; linen tape for textiles; and medium lead pencil for manuscripts and paper objects.

MEASURING

Measuring is important for both identification and for calculating storage or exhibition-space requirements. The measuring equipment should include a folding rule, steel and cloth tapes, a measuring stand, calipers, etc. In general, the dimensions (height, length, width, depth, and diameter) are all taken at the greatest point.

CLASSIFIED ACCESSION REGISTER (CAR)

Smaller museums may have only General Accession Register but big museums maintain two types of register (1) General Accession Register, and (2) Classified Accession Register. While GAR has necessarily to be only one in a museum, CAR can be many, depending upon the types of collection in the museum. CAR has the same columns as the GAR. The columns of photograph and its negative no. are added in CAR. Further, in CAR the object is described in detail.

INDEX CARD

This is also called "pubic record." Small museums have only one set of index cards but big museums can have five types of index cards.

1. Accession Card
2. Object Card
3. Material Card
4. Location Card
5. Find-spot Card

The size of each card is generally 3" × 5". The quality of the card should be very good in terms of thickness and smoothness since these are for permanent and repeated use. Photograph must also be pasted on the backside of the cards, if not all the types, then at least the Accession Card. These cards can be purchased in the market very easily.

Accession Card

it should bear the following:

Accession No.	Location
Object	Material
Date	Find-spot
Dimensions	Photo-negative no.
Published reference	

Other four types of cards should have the same information except the extra desired information which may be written on the top.

CATALOGUE CARD AND PRINTED CATALOGUE

This is a final document of a museum. This is totally for public. Anyone can consult it, including the researchers. A Catalogue Card is the card which contains the gist of all the museum records relating to a particular museum object. The headings of Index card can be repeated on the Catalogue Card but with a lot of space for detailed description and published references.

A set of catalogue cards are known as "catalogue book." Catalogue book, or simply Catalogue, should be printed, if possible, on art paper with excellent colour photographs of objects. Every object listed in it should have not only detailed description of its physical entity but also its scholarly analysis. It establishes the credibility of the museum curators in the world of scholarship. Every Catalogue Card and every printed and published catalogue should at least have one fairly big photograph of the object although these days the published catalogue contain several details of the objects through several photographs.

Exhibition

Exhibition of museum objects for public at large is the primary function of a museum. Modern museums are not simply the "store houses of curios." Public money is used by the museum authorities to do their jobs. Hence they owe a great responsibility towards them.

There are five types of exhibitions —

1. Permanent or gallery exhibitions
2. Temporary or periodic exhibitions
3. Special exhibitions which could be even thematic
4. Educational exhibition
5. Circulating exhibition

PERMANENT OR GALLERY EXHIBITION

Permanent galleries can be considered as key-galleries which speak for the richness of a particular museum collection. In these, the best representatives of the collection are exhibited to satisfy the aesthetic, scientific and scholarly urges of the visitors and also to fulfil their desire of seeing the rare, the unique and the beautiful objects. Though the permanent galleries must show the representative collection, it is not necessary to fill these with examples of each and every type of object and make them crowded in the showcases. These galleries should have only the best and very important specimens. These should be properly illuminated and attractively presented to capture the attention of the visitors. The labels in them should have the element of what is called "all the basic information." The galleries should have as far as possible thematic exhibitions.

TEMPORARY OR PERIODIC EXHIBITIONS

These exhibitions are not permanent exhibitions but are organized in order to bring out important objects in the "reserve collection" of the museum so that the visitors will have a chance to see the collection which is not normally on view. These exhibitions are mounted only for short periods of time, from a few months to a few weeks or even days. This gives an opportunity to visitors to see many examples of the same period or the same school of art at a time and allow them to make a comparative study.

SPECIAL OR THEMATIC EXHIBITIONS

These exhibitions can be considered as an extension to the periodic exhibitions. It is not necessary to limit the periodic exhibitions only to a particular type or school of a particular archaeological collection for example. Some of these can be planned as thematic exhibitions which are meant for the comparative study on a wider scale of bringing together objects of different schools and periods depicting a particular theme. This would enlighten public in knowing how a particular art or festival or a deity has been represented, survived or changed though different arts or different regions or different media or through the development of sciences.

EDUCATIONAL EXHIBITIONS

The educational exhibitions are planned with the purpose of educating the visitors by "all means", and use all the aids like illustrations, charts, photographs, replicas, touch-screen computers, etc. The educational exhibition can be considered as demonstrative or illustrative exhibition where the sole purpose is to give information, making use of all aids, so that the particular techniques of creating the object are fully learnt by the visitors as such learning would help them to understand other collections.

CIRCULATING EXHIBITIONS

Circulating exhibitions are also known as "travelling exhibitions." Circulating exhibitions can be utilised by other institutions and museums which sometimes can and may share the expenses and get the benefit of the work done by showing the exhibition in their institutions. It may be only of objects mounted on panels which can be easily packed or unpacked and can be set up for purposes of exhibitions in any sheltered place. All captions, labels should be planned or incorporated in the panel itself so that no work has to be done at the site of the exhibition. It is also possible to arrange such exhibitions in a vehicle, in a bus, or trailer which can travel from place to place. The slogan is "if people cannot come to the museum, let the museum go to them." There are "Mobile Exhibitions" and the buses containing them are "Museum Buses."

Display or Presentation Techniques

Museum collections, when put on display, presently called "presentation" since "display" is the term used in markets to attract people for commercial purposes and not for sober presentation. These should have special attention paid to following items since they make the objects speak for themselves.

LIGHTING

Light brings out the character of objects if used in an effective way. It brightens the three-dimensional objccts, sculptures, and builds an attractive atmosphere around the object. There are two types of museum lighting — "natural lighting" and "artificial lighting." It is advisable to blend both the sources of light to get the desirable and useful mixed light. However, the natural light should be avoided if the objects are natural in origin since ultraviolet rays can destroy such objects. The amount of light and its quality for galleries have to be considered in relation to contrast, glare, colour effects, colour of light, brightness of object and room lighting. Good contrast of brightness is desirable for satisfactory visibility. Eyes can easily focus on a good contrast, but strong contrast is tiring and confusing. Light coming from one direction gives a sharp contrast. It is better to have light from two or more directions with predominance of light from one top-left or top-right at 45° angle. Lighting should be controlled through "Lux-meters" which record the intensity of the gallery. It should be sufficient so that the objects are visible but light should not be glaring to the eyes of the visitors. The source of the light should not be visible to the visitor's eyes directly as it gives an irritating glare. Indirect and reflected light gives good and subdued light for general lighting. When displayed in a showcase, the object must be seen brighter than its surroundings so that it attracts the attention of the visitor. It must also be noted that objects of different materials need different intensities of light, for example, miniature paintings cannot be exposed to light more than 150 lux.

BACKGROUND

Background plays a very important part in the presentation of art objects in the showcases and galleries. The colour scheme and texture of the background cloth or paper should be selected keeping in mind the richness, texture and form of the object. The background should, it may be noted, be able to bring out the characteristics of the objects shown against them. The object should be prominent against the background and not the background itself. In order to avoid repetition, colour-schemes should be changed from gallery to gallery.

FURNITURE

All the objects in the museum cannot be presented in one and the same manner. Some of them need their placement on the wall, some have to be seen from all sides, and others need protection from weather as well as from visitors. To accommodate such a vast variety of objects requiring different kinds of treatment, pedestals, low platforms with or without glass-cases, wall-cases, wall-shelves, and table-cases are needed. Designs of all these should be in harmony and well suited to the purpose. Movable screens and partitions are also helpful in creating additional wall space and small limited enclosures.

4

Museum Architecture

THERE is nothing like an ideal plan for museum building which will serve any type of museum. However, every collection will have its own conditions, requirements, purposes and problems. So the museum authorities and architect have to work in close co-operation, to make the building safe and secured as well as functional and user-friendly with gardens and trees for the most pleasing, inviting and healthy ambience.

Site

The choice of site needs careful consideration. Whenever a site is chosen, first consideration should be of building for the present requirements with provisions for future expansion. It should be easily accessible by the people, hence not too far from the town centre. The building should have enough open space around it, giving good amount of natural light and ventilation.

Functional Areas

The area in the museum building can be divided into two broad categories:

(i) Public Area, and

(ii) Service Area.

Public Area will include the galleries, auditorium, library, cafeteria, etc. while the Service Area is needed for offices of administration and technical staff, store rooms, workshops, air-conditioning plant and electrical installation as well as Conservation Laboratory. In addition to these, there must be provision for toilets and cloak rooms for the public and members of the staff separately and water-rooms for drinking water as well as enough corridors and staircases for free circulation of the visitors.

PLANNING OF PUBLIC AREA

The entrance hall should be a large one, to admit big crowds and should lead to the auditorium, library, sale and ticket-counter without going through the galleries. A museum auditorium should be equipped with a projection room, which is necessary for illustrated lectures as well as showing documentary films. The stage of the auditorium should be suitable for multipurpose activities, including occasional cultural performances. It should have ante-room attached to it which may be used by the lecturer or can be used as a green room for cultural performances. Enquiry and sales counter should be located in entrance hall and should give all the required guidance to the public. Toilet and cloak room should be directly accessible from the entrance hall and should be neat, clean and well-equipped and well-maintained. Staircases and corridors should be wide enough to take a normal crowd. It may be advisable to keep plants in certain corners which can give corridors a pleasant look and provide relief to the visitors against the museum fatigue.

The planning of the galleries is mainly dependent on the type of collection and the lighting needed for the same. The size of the rooms and the height of the ceiling will be determined by the nature and the dimensions of the exhibits. Large wood-work like *ratha*s and huge sculptures need a height of 14 to 20 ft, while the bronze, coins, and jewellery displayed in the showcases, and miniature paintings do not need high-ceiling galleries.

The treatment of the walls makes a lot of difference to a gallery. An uncluttered wall space is the most usable space in a gallery. If the windows are above 8 ft in height, from the floor level, the wall space below is free for exhibition purposes. No electrical fitting should be located on the walls, instead these may be fixed at the skirting level of the floors of the galleries since at that height no exhibit is put on display; it is within a foot high. Walls also act as a background for free standing exhibits. When the walls are to be used for nailing or fixing the exhibits, cement plastered walls are not of much use. It is much better to line them up with wood panelling, painted with the wall colour. It is then easier to change the exhibits without spoiling the walls.

Floor should be easy to keep clean and should be easily washable. The flooring should not absorb any dirt or dust. It should be non-slippery. The colour of the floor should be darker than the walls so that it may not reflect light on the exhibits lined along the walls and showcases. For this reason, white marble should never be used on the floor as it would reflect light on the walls. Instead, red, grey or green granite are much better from every point of view, even strength.

It is essential to plan a relief area after two or three galleries, where the visitor's eye may rest with the natural surroundings and get relief after continually looking at some exhibits. A few seats provided in these areas will relax the visitors and they can continue the round with more enthusiasm. These areas could be lobbies overlooking a little garden or balconies overlooking the landscape.

PLANNING OF SERVICE AREA

Service Area generally occupies from 20 to 40 per cent of total museum area. Service areas are as important as the museum galleries. The Service Area includes conservation laboratory; offices of the director, curators, administrative staff, technical staff; workshop, photography and graphics section, stores for reserve collection, air-conditioning plant, generator room, etc.

Generally, only 20 per cent objects are displayed in the museum galleries, rest is kept in the store. So, the objects which do not find a permanent place in the galleries must find a safe and sheltered place in the store. It is essential to see that the storage places are properly lighted, well ventilated and adequately guarded against deterioration, decay or damage. In short, the museum storage is a safe place for the objects where they are as much cared for as they are in the galleries. It is desirable to arrange storage in such a way that any object can easily be seen and located without moving objects in the front or surrounding the particular object. These stores need big halls and should be near or inside the curator's office. Each object in the store needs proper care and vigilance of the curator. 24 hour air-conditioning is an essential requirement in the storage if it contains organic objects.

For textile, textile-rollers made of aluminium sheets on wooden frame, are used. Each textile is individually rolled. Costumes are not hung on hangers in the almirahs but laid to rest horizontally without any folds. Fragments of wall-paintings, miniature paintings, manuscripts, photographs, etc. are stored in shallow drawers. Three-dimensional objects are stored on the shelves. Small decorative arts objects should be kept in a storage cabinet in a way that each box can slide out independently. Mounted and framed paintings can be hung on sliding frames or stationary partitions. Coins can be stored in a tray with individual grooves for each coin. Such trays can be fitted into a cabinet.

For conservation laboratory, modelling section, workshops and photography section water connection as well as exhaust fans are needed. Photography section needs a small dark room with all the necessary equipment for developing photographs although these days digital cameras are used which do not require a dark room.

5

Museum Security

THE security of museum objects is the primary responsibility of the museum. Proper security must be provided to museum objects against theft and fire. These two are mainly the most hazardous things to museum security.

Security against Theft

Museum must take proper precautions against theft. Some points are given below to prevent theft:

1. There must be only one entrance gate in the museum. This entrance must be properly guarded by at least two guards. These guards must check every visitor as well as staff members of the museum.
2. There must be the provision of cloak room near the entrance where visitors can keep their belongings against tokens but free of charge.
3. There should not be any open water or electricity or drainage pipeline which goes to upper floors. Big trees around the museum building should be avoided. These are the media by which a thief can enter the museum.
4. All the windows which open outside the museum must be covered by grills or bullet-proof glasses.

5. There must be twenty-four hour vigil by the security guards in and around the museum building. The duty must be changed after every eight hours of the duty time.
6. At night, the museum building should be properly lit from all sides. For this flood-lights should be used.
7. Hidden locks must be used in showcases. Precious objects must be put up inside bullet-proof showcases.
8. The security department of the museum is headed by a security officer assisted by armed guards, chowkidars, gallery attendants, etc.
9. At the time of closing the museum every gallery must be sealed with signature of curator and the security officer of the museum. The next day the seal will be opened in the presence of the above-said two officers.
10. There must be a provision of a key room in a museum, with written records of issuing and returning of keys.
11. In case of an international exhibition museum can take the services of BSF (Border Security Force), ITBP (Indo Tibetan Border Police), CRPF (Central Reserve Police Force) and CISF (Central Industrial Security Force), etc.
12. The security officer must take the round of the museum at least four times a day to check all the security measures. He should make surprise visits at night time also.
13. Keeping dog squad provides additional advantage to museum security. These dogs can easily be

obtained from 'Dog Training Centre.' These centres train the dogs in a manner that they may prevent any theft attempt by the burglars. This is very low cost and fool-proof security arrangement. These dogs guard the museum by their extraordinary sniffing power. After closing the museum dogs are deployed in the premises of the museum till the opening of the museum next day. Chandigarh Museum is the best example of this type of security.

Electronic Devices

METAL DETECTOR

This device detects the metal and makes sound. Security guards check every visitor by this device to find out metallic things or arms which may be used to harm the museum object or breaking the glass of the showcase.

C.C.T.V.

By the help of Closed Circuit Television security guards can keep vigil on the galleries of the museum. In this device small movable cameras are installed in the different parts of the museum which record and relay the live video recordings in the control room through television screens.

GLASS-BREAK ALARM

These alarms are fitted in the showcases. If anybody breaks the glass of the showcase then the alarm makes sound.

BURGLAR ALARM

This device is fitted beneath the object, if anybody lifts the object then it sets off an alarm.

MOTION DETECTORS

This device finds out any motion in the gallery. At the time of closing the museum this device should be activated. If anybody enters the gallery it finds him out and makes the alarm ring. There are four types of motion-detectors.

(i) Ultrasonic motion detector;

(ii) Microwave motion detector;

(iii) Infrared motion detector;

(iv) Passive infrared motion detector.

PHOTOELECTRIC BEAM

This device is fitted inside the showcase. When anybody lifts the object the photoelectric beam cuts and the alarm rings.

Security against fire

Fire is the major threat to a museum. Museum might recover stolen items and repair damaged objects but fire destroys quickly and permanently all the organic objects. Some points are given below to prevent fire hazard in museum.

1. Training of museum staff is very essential. Training includes the handling of fire fighting equipment, the phone numbers of fire-fighters, immediately informing the higher authorities, etc.
2. Museum staff must co-operate with firefighters and render all the necessary help to them.
3. Museum should strictly prohibit smoking in its premises. "No Smoking" signs should be installed in

different parts of the museum.

4. Electrical wiring and other electrical instruments should be checked from time to time. Sometimes, short-circuit happens and fire breaks out. Keep a vigil over it so that it does not spread out. "Sand" and "Water," if possible "foam" may be used to extinguish it.

Fire fighting devices

EXTINGUISHERS

There are mainly five types of extinguishers.

(i) *Foam Type* — The foam type of extinguisher, when operated, emits thick foam which covers the fire area and prevents the supply of oxygen. But it is costly.

(ii) *Soda Acid Type* — When the plunger is struck, it breaks the acid phial (bottle). The sulphuric acid and sodium bicarbonate solution react together to release carbon dioxide (CO_2). The CO_2 thus generated creates pressure which forces the water out of the extinguisher. The CO_2 acts only as a propellant and the water extinguishes the fire by cooling effect.

(iii) *C.T.C. Type* — Carbon Tetra Chloride, which is a non-conducting liquid, is used in this type of extinguisher. Carbon Tetra Chloride is vaporized into a gas by the heat of fire and is capable of extinguishing small fires.

(iv) *CO_2 Type* — Carbon-dioxide is a gas but can be liquidized and stored. In this extinguisher liquid carbon dioxide is stored in the cylinder. When it comes out it is converted into gas. It is capable of extinguishing fire by reducing the oxygen supply needed to continue combustion.

(v) *Dry Powder type* — Dry powder type fire extinguishers are suitable for tackling petroleum fires, gas fires, and fires in electrical equipment and for controlling surface fires in textile fibres. These extinguishers are noted for the speed with which they put out fires. The chemical powders employed are usually sodium-based and when applied to a fire, undergo chemical reaction. The free radicals which are responsible for sustaining any fire are put out of action by the dry chemical powders and, because of this, the fire dies out very fast.

FIRE HYDRANT SYSTEM

Fire Hydrant System is the oldest and still one of the most effective techniques. It consists of a sufficiently large water reservoir, fire pump sets (main and standby), jockey pump set, hydrant valves, fire-fighting hoses, and branch pipes with nozzles. This is a semi-automatic system. A network of pipes is laid out, depending upon the risk, with hydrant valves placed at strategic places. The spacing/distance between yard hydrants are guided by norms, viz. the entire pipeline is kept pressurized with water. Whenever anyone opens a hydrant valve, the pressure in the pipeline reduces drastically and jockey pump set, which normally keeps the total system pressurized, is unable to cope with the system demand which results in further fall in pressure. The further fall in pressure is sensed by the designated pressure switch which automatically starts the main fire pump set. Depending upon the type and sensitivity of the risk, diesel-engine powered fire pump set should also be installed having 100 per cent standby capacity.

WATER SPRINKLER SYSTEM

A sprinkler system consists of a water supply (or supplies) and one or more sprinkler installations. Each installation consists of a set of installation control valves and a pipe array fitted with sprinkler heads. The sprinkler heads are fitted at specified locations at the roof or ceiling, and where necessary between racks, below shelves, inside ovens or stoves or below obstructions. A sprinkler has two functions to perform. It must first detect a fire, and must then provide an adequate distribution of water to control or extinguish it. Each function is performed separately and one is independent of the other except in so far as early detection makes extinction easier because the fire has not grown large.

HALON RELEASE UNIT

Areas housing very high value collection deserves a high level of fire protection. Helon 1301 system uses a halon gas as an extinguishing agent. It is almost the same as the water sprinkler system but here helon gas is stored in a huge cylinder instead of water.

FIRE DETECTION AND ALARM SYSTEM

These are the devices by which museum authorities can detect fire and find out the accurate location of fire.

(i) *Thermal Detector* — This alarm uses a thermistor which is coupled to an electronic circuit housed in a package which can be mounted on ceiling. It responds to change of temperature near it and sets off an alarm when the ambient temperature rises above a certain point.

(ii) *Smoke Detector* — It gives an alarm when smoke from a fire enters in this system.

(iii) *Fire Repeater Panel* — It is placed in each and every floor and gallery. This panel indicates the zone or gallery or area of fire.

(iv) *Fire Hooter* — The hooter is activated by heat and it makes sound automatically.

6

Museum Marketing

MUSEUM Marketing is a philosophy which provide useful guidelines to a museum regarding how to raise income, how to provide better services to visitors, how to enhance primary resources, how to popularize the museum among masses, how to fulfil newly developed needs of visitors, etc.; in other words, Museum Marketing is a tool which helps a museum to achieve its goal.

There are four important components of any type of marketing, which are:

1. Product,
2. Consumer,
3. Promotion,
4. Profit.

Museum Product

Museum building, artefacts, special exhibitions, different kinds of services, facilities and programmes, which are related to the masses, are the products of the museum. It does not mean that museum artefacts and other things are on sale in the museum. A museum does not sell its artefacts, it always acquires and preserves them for the future. However, all these museum products are experienced by the senses (i.e. seeing, touching, operating, hearing, thinking, enjoying, etc.) of visitors. Museum products (services, activities and programmes) can be classified into following parts:

(i) Education services (such as lectures, seminars, gallery talks, film shows, etc.).

(ii) Information services (such as proper labels, detailed description of the subject, guide services, audio-video aid, etc.).

(iii) Exhibitions (permanent, temporary and special).

(iv) Conservation and proper upkeep of heritage.

(v) Visitor services (drinking water, toilet facility, proper orientation, etc.).

(vi) Supporting research activities and disseminate it to visitors.

(vii) Museum fairs and festivals.

(viii) Performance programmes (dance, drama, song, etc.).

(ix) Workshops for teachers and children.

(x) Museum corners and school loan services.

(xi) Publications (brochures, guidebook, catalogue, gallery sheet, handbook, etc.).

The above-mentioned products (services) of the museum should not only be of very good quality but also the maintenance of that quality is also very much required. The quality of service may be seen from the user's viewpoint and not the museum's. The staff or employees of the museum, who are co-ordinators of all museum products (services), should be well trained to handle the museums services and be cooperative with the visitors.

The core of marketing is "competition." So, many museums are trying to attract more visitors, more collection, more income, more volunteers, more government grants, more donation, more projects, more fame, etc. so, a kind of competition exists among museums. But, it must be healthy competition and one museum should not defame the other museums. However, competition motivates museum to do better, i.e. provide better services to visitors, better display, better environment, better education system, better publication, etc.

Consumer

The consumers of the museum are visitors, who invest their time, money (in the form of buying ticket, transportation, etc.), energy, etc. and in return the museum should provide best facilities to them. For this purpose, segmentation (or classification of its visitors in smaller groups) is very much needed because different groups of people need different types of treatment such as school children, adults, housewives, semi-literate, illiterate, highly-literate, ethnic minority, physically and mentally challenged people, foreigners, etc. So, it is the responsibility of the museum to cater to or fulfil the needs of all the segments of the society. Ideally a museum should offer everything to everybody but it is just not possible, still it may have many things to offer to all visitors. If a museum divides its visitors into smaller groups, it can certainly cater to their needs precisely and logically.

Museum should also see whether the products (programmes and services) which are offered to the consumers (visitors) are effective or not, and consumers are benefited by the services or not. These things can be found out by consumer's research — qualitative and quantitative. In a qualitative research, what the consumer feels about a museum product is noted. In quantitative research, data surveys are done on the consumers to find out four key information:

(i) Level of Use — What galleries are visited most and what are not and on which days and time.

(ii) Characteristics of Visit — Journey time, journey distance, form of transport, the route, parking facilities, etc.

(iii) Characteristics of the Consumers — Their age, educational background, purpose behind the museum visit, etc.

(iv) Publicity Information — What newspapers and magazines do the consumers read, what T.V. programmes do they like most, etc.

Personal interviews, remarks on the visitor's book, watching the behaviour of the visitor and questionnaire are some of the ways to collect information about visitors. The main purpose behind getting these details about the consumers is to find out the problems and complications by which consumers are not able to avail the services of the museum properly.

The main aim of the museum is to see that visitors return

from the museum with full satisfaction and come next time soon with their friends, family and relatives.

Promotion

Promotion is a key factor of marketing which acts as a bridge between the products and the consumers. By the help of promotion consumers (visitors) get to know about the museum and its products (services). In other words, promotion is a medium of attracting visitors to the museum. Promotion can be done by the following methods:

(i) *Personal Selling* — It is rightly said that "all the museum staff are ambassadors of the museum." Each and every member of the museum staff can contribute in his/her own way to promote the museum. The museum staff should be trained enough, be polite and well co-operative in order to leave a positive impact on the visitors' mind. Visitors are impressed by all these and tell their well-wishers about the museum. So, by this the popularity of the museum inceases day by day.

(ii) *Museum Literature* — Museum literatures are used to promote a museum among masses. Museum literature such as brochures, leaflets, posters, guidebooks, gallery sheets, stickers, catalogues, etc. are used for that purpose. These literature provide an overview of museum artefacts, its services, activities, programmes, etc. to visitors.

(iii) *Advertising* — It is an expensive but a powerful medium of promoting a museum. Museum can take the services of newspapers, magazines, radio, television, etc. to promote itself. Inviting press and mass media people on certain important occasion like opening ceremony of a temporary/special exhibition, opening of a new museum gallery, organizing museum fairs and festivals, celebrating Museum Day, Children's Day, Environment Day, etc. and to brief media persons about the event and organize press conferences, besides press releases on such occasions, increase the popularity of a museum among masses.

(iv) *Public Relations* — Public relations is the practice of managing the flow of information between the museum and its visitors. Telephonic conversation, face-to-face conversation, conversation through e-mail, letters, website, contact with people through newspapers, magazines, radio, TV, films, news, etc. are the mediums of marketing relations with the public. These are the methods by which a museum can establish and maintain goodwill and promote itself among masses.

(v) *Word of Mouth* — "Word of mouth" is the best publicity method that a museum can rely upon. The main reason behind this thinking is that "a satisfied visitor will send ten others to the museum." For this, a museum should look at each and every requirement of the visitors and try to fulfil these requirements so that every visitor may return from the museum with some special feelings.

Profit (Income Generation)

ICOM while defining a museum clearly mentions it as a "non-profit making institution." So, it is a prime quality of a museum not to make any profit. But for managing and maintaining such a huge infrastructure of a museum, a lot of fund is required and one cannot depend merely on government grant which is not enough for proper functioning of a museum. Museums have to generate their own income, not for making profit but to execute their services, programmes, and activities properly. There are a lot of methods by which a museum can generate its income. These are:

(i) *Entry Fee* — Museum's income can be generated by entry ticket. Museums should also fix tickets for still camera and video camera separately to generate more income. Some museums take a huge amount from foreigners as entry fee to generate more income. Some museums take separate entry fee for special or temporary exhibition.

(ii) *Museum Shop* — Museum publication, CDs, DVDs, other publication on art and culture, plaster casts, decorative art objects, etc. should be on sale in museum shop. It will also generate income.

(iii) *Museum Cafeteria* — Museum cafeteria should be neat and clean and well maintained for museum visitors. Fresh food, snacks, tea, coffee, cold drinks, etc. should be available all the time and served to visitors against payment. It will also provide some additional income to the museum.

(iv) *Hiring the Facilities* — Museums has huge resources that can be utilized by corporate organizations or business groups against payment. Hiring its air-conditioned auditorium, conference hall, lush green garden, parking space, etc. for workshops, musical concerts, launching a product, etc. would fetch a lot of money.

(v) *Loan of Collection* — Museum can charge some amount against providing some of its collection as a loan to other museums or organizations for a specific period.

(vi) *Museum Consultancy* — Museums can send their curators, assistant curators, technical assistants, electricians, carpenters, painters, etc. to other museums or organizations for consultancy or technical assistance or providing them some useful guidelines and tips. Sometimes museum's advice is taken to identify or test an object. Museum can charge for all these services to generate income.

(vii) *Special Cultural Programmes* — Sometimes special cultural programmes on dance, drama, music performances by renowned artists are organized by the museum. Income through ticket money will also raise the revenue of the museum.

(viii) *Donation* — Museum should contact wealthy persons, corporate bodies, rich organizations and encourage them to give donation to the museum not only in the form of money but also gifts like computers, furniture, showcases, ACs, etc. or volunteered time. Once a museum convinces its donors about the proper use of their donation, money may be obtained easily. Donors have to be treated well and given certain special privileges such as private viewing, free entry, discount on museum publications and other objects on museum shop, etc.

(ix) *Sponsorship* — Many big firms or individuals or organizations may come forward to sponsor museum events, programmes, activities, and services for the following reasons:

(A) To publicize and promote the brand name of the company.

(B) To improve the general image of the company.

(C) To build a kind of relationship with the clients and influential people.

(D) To develop good relationship with consumers and local community.

(E) To save tax money.

Museum should try to build long-term relationship with sponsors and donors. However, sponsorship should be carefully handled with a distance being kept between the museum and the sponsor. Sponsorship should be fruitful for both the parties. A museum need not abandon its interests under the pressure of a sponsor.

7

Museum Orientation

WHEN a visitor comes to a museum, he knows nothing about a museum, he does not find his way inside the museum building, he does not find his favourite object in a museum, he does not find cafeteria or rest rooms in a museum, he does not find his way out of a building, he does not find the place where to park his car, etc. All these types of visitor-related matters are solved under the subject of Museum Orientation. Orientation problems do not start from the front gate of a museum. They begin long before when a visitor plans for a museum visit at his home and he does not know where the museum is, what is the route to reach the museum, which public transport is needed to reach the museum, and what is the entry fee and timing of a museum.

The problems of orientation can be divided into six parts. Each part can be discussed individually. These are:

1. Pre-visit orientation,
2. Arrival orientation/Psychological orientation,
3. Orientation during support facilities/Wayfinding,
4. Circulation,
5. Orientation during exhibit viewing/Intellectual Orientation,

6. Exit Orientation.

Pre-Visit Orientation

Orientation begins with the images and messages that inform the public of the existence and location of a particular museum and encourage them to visit a museum with a preconception. Generally, these topics are discussed under the study of pre-visit orientation:

1. Location of visitors,
2. Types of transport,
3. Distance to be travelled,
4. Availability of transport,
5. Expenses on transport,
6. Time spent on travelling,
7. Knowledge of museum,
8. Entry ticket,
9. Appeal of subject,
10. Facilities/services available,
11. Accessibility,
12. Previous visit,
13. Previous experience,
14. Weather,
15. Time of year,
16. Available time,
17. Interest level/range,
18. Family members of visitors.

Transport and media are the most important components of pre-visit orientation, which can be discussed separately.

TRANSPORT

It is the museum's responsibility to arrange transport facility to the public. For this the museum can contact tour operators and request them to include the museum visit in the tour programme. Tour operators have their own buses. Museums should also run their own buses on different routes to feed museums with visitors. These buses should also go to schools, and school children may be brought to the museum for a visit.

Museum should also put milestones and arrow labels on key locations so that visitors could easily reach the museum. Some museums (like Kurukshetra Museum, etc.) have introduced the milestone system. There should be proper space for parking in the vicinity of the museum.

The locational map for reaching the museum and bus route numbers should be clearly mentioned in the brochures, tickets and other publications of the museum.

MEDIA

Museums can orient their visitors by the help of advertising and publicity media. Foreign museums are using full page of daily newspapers to provide primary information about the museum to the public. Museums are easily accessible on internet, which provides all the necessary information to the people like location, transport, route, timing, entry fee, services and facilities, etc. Museum can use different types of media, for providing various information and programmes of the museum to the public, which are being mentioned below:

1. *Newspapers* — Daily, weekly, weekend, colour magazines, domestic, foreign, international, news stories, features, photographs, editorials, letters, advertising, advertising features.
2. *Magazines* — Weekly, monthly, quarterly, annual, occasional, domestic, foreign, international, general readership, special readership groups, trade/ commerce.
3. *Television* — Features, news stories, interviews, documentaries, talk shows, quizzes, advertising.
4. *Radio* — Features, news stories, interviews, documentaries, talk shows, quizzes, advertising.
5. *Printed materials* — Posters, leaflets, direct mail, brochures, letters, information fliers, banner/flags, advertising fliers.
6. Display shops, travel centres, cultural centres, fairs and festivals, promotional events.

Arrival Orientation/Psychological Orientation

There are three major elements of arrival orientation:

(i) Parking,

(ii) Finding the entrance,

(iii) Entrance orientation.

Parking of a vehicle is really a problem in metropolitan cities. Many people are discouraged from visiting a museum because of parking difficulties. To solve this problem, there should be a big parking space in the vicinity of a museum with proper directions, signages and necessary information.

Finding the entrance can be difficult as big museums are having multiple doors but only one of which is the correct entrance for visitors. The entrance should be clearly marked with some direction signs to avoid confusion among the visitors.

A visitor enters into a museum with tiredness, exhaustion, confusion, etc. and he/she needs relaxation, calm and receptive mood before he or she enters the museum galleries. The design and facilities (like toilet, drinking water, etc.) of the museum's entrance hall (also called orientation area) will greatly change the mood of the visitors and they will find themselves refreshed and psychologically fit to visit museum galleries. A well maintained reception counter and information desk should be located just near the entrance. Staff of these counters must possess all the necessary information about the museum and should be capable of answering all the questions of visitors.

Orientation to Support Facilities or Wayfinding

Sometimes visitors get frustrated for not being able to locate museum facilities like washrooms (toilets), library, museum sales shop, cafeteria, auditorium, seminar room, conference hall, etc. Wayfinding or topographical or locational orientation has a great role in solving this problem. Orientation devices such as maps, direction signs and signages provide great help to visitors for locating different places. "YOU-ARE-HERE" maps which tell the visitors where he/she is right now, provide useful piece of information.

Circulation

Circulation describes how visitors make their way through the museum. Which pathways do visitors adopt in the museum? Do visitors circulate in the same way that the designers intended? Do visitors miss key exhibits because of the architectural design of the museum? Which direction do visitors turn when they reach their desired place? Do visitors have a circulation strategy (e.g. to turn right and follow the parameter)? Do visitors simply roam about more or less aimlessly? Orientation will influence the circulation pattern of visitors and provide them appropriate path to visit museum properly.

Orientation during Exhibit Viewing or Intellectual Orientation

Visitors need proper orientation to see the museum exhibits in detail and understand the key features of the objects. There are some orientation techniques which provide complete knowledge about museum artefacts:

1. Texts and labels (the most widely used method).
2. Printed catalogue, guidebook, gallery sheets, bulletins, etc.
3. Use of room settings, dioramas, models, etc. to present objects in context.
4. Use of photographs, maps, drawings, etc. to present object in detail.

5. Audio-visual enhancements like head phones, speakers, slide tapes, videos, multimedia and computer systems, etc.
6. Guide lectures to provide useful information about objects.
7. Dance, drama, song performances and storytelling to provide great source of information about tribal or regional cultures and objects.
8. Fairs and festivals.
9. Museum's scheduled tours, demonstrations, special events, lectures, film shows, gallery talk, courses, etc.
10. Access to the museum's reserve collection, library, modelling section, laboratory and other resources.

Exit Orientation

Sometimes visitors do not find their way to the exit. Sometimes, visitors want to see only one gallery or exhibition then they want to go back. While going, they may face problems locating exit doors. To resolve this problem museum should use "EXIT" sign at different places of the museum. Maps of the museum and "YOU-ARE-HERE" maps are also useful to find the exit.

While leaving the museum and going to their home back some visitors may face the problem of transportation. To resolve this problem museum should guide visitors and provide them information about the route, transportation, taxi/auto stand, bus stand, etc.

8

Museum Evaluation

EVALUATION is the key to ensure whether services or projects or activities undertaken by the museum are effective or not, and whether visitors are gaining something from it or not. By evaluation museums get to know to what extent they are popular among the masses, to what extent people are making use of its services, how many people come to visit the museum and how many are not coming to it, how to attract those people who are not coming to the museum. We also get to know which segment of the society comes to museum and which segment does not come to the museum. By evaluation we also know what people expect from the museum, what people do not like in the museum, why visitors are not coming to see the museum again and again. We also know if the museum is providing adequate facilities to visitors.

There are three kinds of evaluation:

1. Front end Evaluation,
2. Formative Evaluation, and
3. Summative Evaluation.

Front end Evaluation

Whenever the museum starts planning any new project or

programme, front end evaluation provides inputs and basic information to the museum. Front end evaluation shows the path to the museum and provides useful guidelines, regarding how to develop a programme in an appropriate manner at the very beginning. For front end evaluation, target or potential audience is called to the museum to examine their existing knowledge about the programme and to grasp their useful thoughts and suggestions regarding the development of programme. For example, if a museum is planning an exhibition then by front end evaluation the museum can get so much useful information from the target audience, such as what would be the theme of the exhibition, what would be the name of the exhibition, what are the objects required for the exhibition, which type of audio-visual aid and information panel would be required for the exhibition, what would be the expectations of the visitors, etc.

Formative Evaluation

Formative evaluation provides useful information and guidelines to the museum to improve the programme while it is in the process of development. In other words, by formative evaluation a detailed study is done with the help of target audience to find out whether a programme, which is currently being undertaken by the museum, is fulfilling its aims, objectives and goals or not, and if it lacks, what are the lacunae behind it. Formative evaluation provides answers to all such questions. For example, if a museum is in the process of organizing a temporary exhibition, then by formative evaluation the museum can get so much valuable information from the target audience like what impact the exhibition is providing right now and what more improvements are required to make it more effective, what should be the sequence of the objects, which colour would be more appropriate for a background, what key information should be on the information boards, how to make the display more beautiful, how to blend mock-ups and dioramas with the exhibition so that display may look more powerful, so on and so forth.

Summative Evaluation

The purpose of a summative evaluation is to assess the effectiveness of the programme. Summative evaluation is done to find out whether the programme has achieved its predefined aims, objectives and goals or not. It also finds out the overall impact of the programme on visitors (positive or negative and to what extent) and whether the needs of those who are served by the programme have been fulfilled or not. For example, in case of a temporary exhibition, visitors are asked such questions as to what extent they like or dislike the exhibition, what are the things they like most, what are the things they dislike most, what impact (direct or indirect, short term or long term) the exhibition has on them, to what extent changes have occurred on the visitor's understanding, attitude, emotions and behaviors after seeing the exhibition, etc.

Methods of Evaluation

Evaluation studies may be of two types — qualitative and quantitative. The main objective of both qualitative and quantitative studies is to pinpoint the factors responsible for the success or failure of the programme. In qualitative studies, the evaluator takes the opinion of a relatively small number of individuals while in quantitative studies the evaluator carries out the study on a large number of individuals and on a wider scale.

Target Audience

Before evaluation process starts, evaluators must select their target audience or the individuals on whom the study will be done. These individuals may belong to the different sections of the society. They may be school children, college students, research scholars, lay persons, office going people, old people, housewives, businessmen, politicians, etc.

Type of Evaluation

There may be five ways of doing evaluation:

1. Questionnaire,
2. Interview,
3. Projective Studies,
4. Visitors Observations,
5. Visitor's Book.

QUESTIONNAIRE

Questionnaire consists of a fixed schedule of questions which the respondent is expected to answer. This requires a direct effort on the part of the respondent to write in the necessary information sheet. The design of an effective questionnaire requires a lot of ingenuity and consideration on the part of the evaluator. While designing a questionnaire the evaluator must keep three things in his mind — (i) nature of queries, (ii) relevance of queries, and (iii) answering capabilities of the respondent.

There can be two types of questionnaire: (i) objective type questionnaire, and (ii) subjective type questionnaire. The answer of objective type questionnaire can be very brief or just one word, while the answer of subjective type questionnaire can be descriptive or may have a few lines. Questionnaire can be prepared in so many ways:

1. *Yes/No Type Questions*

This is a very easy type of questionnaire. The format of this type of questionnaire is:

(i) Have you visited this museum before — Yes/No,

(ii) Have you gone to the auditorium to see the film show — Yes/No.

2. *Number Scale Type Questions*

In this questionnaire, visitors are asked to give points to the museum programme on a scale of 1 to 5 where 1 is not interesting at all and 5 is very interesting. The format of this type of questionnaire can be

(i) Have you liked this exhibit in an exhibition

1	2	3	4	5

3. *Rating Scale Type Questions*

Rating scale type questions are put to visitors to find out the effectiveness of the museum services. The format of this type of questionnaire can be:

(i) How would you rate our cafeteria ?

Very good	Good	Average	Poor	Very poor

(ii) How would you rate our film show

Very good	Good	Average	Poor	Very poor

4. Scale of Agreement Type Questions

In this type of questionnaire a few statements are given to visitors for their comments. For example:

	Strongly agree	Agree	Neither agree nor disagree	Disagree	Strongly disagree
Statement 1					
Statement 2					
Statement 3					
Statement 4					

INTERVIEW

Interview is a conversation between the evaluator and the visitor. Interviews are generally on a one-to-one basis, though occasional group discussions may also be used. Interview must be recorded (audio or video) so that its analysis may be done later on. There are three types of interviews:

1. Unstructured interview,
2. Semi-structured interview,
3. Structured interview.

Unstructured Interview

Unstructured interview is a method of interview where questions can be changed or adapted to meet the visitor's intelligence, understanding and belief. Unstructured interviews do not offer a limited, pre-set range of answers for a visitor to choose from, but instead advocate listening to how each individual person responds to the question.

Semi-structured Interview

A semi-structured interview is flexible in nature and allows new questions to be brought up during the interview on the basis of what the visitor says. The evaluator in a semi-structured interview generally has a framework of themes to be explored.

Structured Interview

Structured interview is the one where a visitor is expected to answer the queries on a fixed pattern, the questions and their occurrence remaining precise for all the visitors. The success of such an interview depends greatly on the design of the questionnaire. Such interviews give very precisely relevant data for analysing.

PROJECTIVE STUDIES

Projective studies are done to evaluate the objective of the relevant exhibit or exhibition or museum. These studies involve a psychological exercise wherein the visitor's perception is gauged. Such studies may be carried on a variety of patterns and formats such as:

(i) *Pre-test* — Pre-test is done on visitors before they look at an exhibit or exhibition or museum. The main purpose behind this test is to judge current knowledge of the visitor about that exhibit or exhibition or museum.

(ii) *Post-test* — Post-test is conducted to determine the exact gain in knowledge of the visitor due to the influence of an exhibit or exhibition or museum. An analysis of such a test shows the influence of the exhibit or exhibition or museum on the visitor.

(iii) *Retention test* — Retention test is conducted on visitor after the museum visit, preferably after a few days, to determine the long-term effect and retention level of the communication received from the exhibit or exhibition or museum.

VISITOR'S OBSERVATION

Visitor's observation is also a good technique of evaluation. Visitor's behaviour is observed in the gallery or museum. Visitor's level of interest is also measured in this study. At the time of visitor's observation these points should be monitored carefully:

(i) How a visitor reacts while seeing an object (shouts, groans, laughter, gesture)?

(ii) How he moves in the gallery (route followed, picking up the exhibits to see in detail)?

(iii) Which information labels are read by visitors in detail and how he reads (reading out loud, reading in silence, reading full label, reading half label)?

(iv) What is the visitor's physical interaction while seeing the exhibit (pointing, touching, operating, etc.)?

(v) Which kind of aid the visitor takes while seeing the museum (museum guide, museum literature, film show, audio tour, etc.)?

(vi) Which services the visitor uses in the museum (museum shop, cafeteria, toilet, etc.)?

VISITOR'S BOOK

Visitor's book is the easiest option of evaluation. Visitors write their comments on the museum (its artefacts, services, programmes, etc.) in the visitor's book. At least four columns (name, complete address of the visitor with phone no. and e-mail id, comments, and signature) should be in the visitor's book. Visitor's book not only provides valuable comments of visitors but also gives their address for detailed evaluation, so evaluator can contact the visitors either personally or on phone or by post or by e-mail.

9

Museum Communication

COMMUNICATION is the process of transferring information from a sender to a receiver with the use of a medium in which the communicated information is understood by both sender and receiver. In museum perspective (it is said that) Museum Communication is a study of methods by which a museum interacts with the people, not only those who come to the museum but also those who do not come to the museum. We can divide the whole museum communication into two parts:

1. Museum Communication inside the museum,
2. Museum Communication outside the museum.

Museum Communication inside the Museum

There are so many methods by which a museum communicates to the visitors in the museum:

1. Guide Service,
2. Film Shows,
3. Publication,
4. Information Labels,
5. Audio Devices (Headphone/Interactive Buttons),
6. Gallery Talk,

7. Diorama and Models,
8. Touch Screen Computers,
9. Museum Library,
10. Museum Shop.

Guide Service

Guide service is the best communication medium in the museum. Guides explain the things in a better way. It is a two-way communication process between the museum and the visitors. Guide can clearly see whether a visitor is understanding (listening carefully) the things in the proper way or not. If there is any problem in communication a trained guide may detect it and solve the problem. In this type of communication a visitor can put his query to the guide and get the answer. The language of the guide should be effective and clear but easy to understand. There are so many illiterate people in India, who also come to the museum. While literate people read the information label to understand about the museum and its artefacts, the illiterate people cannot read the labels of the museum. So, it is a great responsibility of a guide to take care of their needs and also disseminate some knowledge to them about the museum and its artefacts.

Film Show

Film show is also a very powerful medium of communication in the museum. Film show provides unique audio/video information to visitors regarding the history of the museum, its key artefacts, their relevance to the history, their significant features, etc. in a very interesting manner. Film show can be done either in auditorium (by the projector) or just outside the gallery (by big screen television with the help of VCD/DVD player).

Museum Publication

Publication occupies a very respectable position in communication. By publication, the museum presents its artefacts and associated information in a very effective manner among the visitors. There are so many kinds of publications, such as:

(i) *Museum Calendar* — It is a very interesting publication of museum. It normally consists of 12 pages, while on every page a big photograph of a well-known museum object is printed. Just below the photograph, a monthly calendar should appear. On the back side of every month's calendar the activities of the museum of that particular month (like temporary exhibitions, gallery talks, seminars, etc.) should be mentioned clearly with date and time. Museum calendar can be published in three different sizes — wall calendar, table calendar and pocket calendar.

(ii) *Picture Postcard* — Picture postcard consists of a postcard size photograph of a famous museum object with very brief information about the photograph and the museum is given on the back side. It is a very important tool which spreads the popularity of the museum and its artefacts among the masses all over the world in a unique way.

(iii) *Brochure* — Brochure provides brief information about the museum, its galleries and its services to the visitors. It also consists of some small size photographs of some key objects of the museum. Brochure is also equipped with the map of the museum which displays the location of all the galleries and other areas of the museum.

(iv) *Gallery Sheet* — Gallery sheet provides brief information about a particular gallery with some photographs of important objects.

(v) *Guidebook or Handbook* — Guidebook introduces the museum, its galleries and key objects to visitors in detail. Guidebook consists of some good quality photographs of important objects.

(vi) *Catalogue* — Catalogue is a very important publication of a museum. Catalogue carries detailed description of some important objects with super quality photographs. The representative collection from each gallery or section of the museum should find its place in the catalogue.

(vii) *Bulletin* — Museum activities, future activities, research done by the museum, new finding, new acquisition, etc. are published in bulletins. There can be four types of bulletin — monthly, quarterly, biannually and annually.

(viii) *Other Publications* — Yearbooks, proceedings, memoirs, monographs, annals, and journals are the other publications of a museum which are highly academic in nature. General visitors have nothing to do with these kinds of publications but such publications are highly beneficial for the research scholars and students who are pursuing higher education.

Information Label

Exhibits or collections of museum directly communicate to visitors with the help of labels. Labels provide basic information to visitors about the exhibits in a unique way. Every museum object must be accompanied by a label. There are two kinds of labels:

(i) Object label, and

(ii) Gallery label.

Object label provides the information of a particular object only. This type of label basically consists of five key information regarding an object such as:

1. Name of the object (such as Ganesha),
2. Material of the object (such as Stone),
3. Date of the object (such as third century CE),
4. Place of the object (such as Kaushambi),
5. Accession No. (such as 99.6).

Gallery label provides a brief introduction of that particular gallery namely the significant features of the collection, their nature, brief history of the collection, key objects of the collection, etc. The size of gallery label is comparatively bigger than the object label.

Audio Devices

In museums, visitors are also provided an audio tour to communicate to them various information about museum collection. The main advantage of the audio device is that it communicates about museum collection to visitors in their own language. Foreigners as well as people from other states of India also come to see the museum. This device provides them information in their own language such as French, German, Russian, Chinese, Tamil, Telugu, Kannada, Malayalam, etc. Museums may use this audio device in two ways

(i) Headphones, and

(ii) Speakers.

Headphones are given to the visitors at the time of their entry into the museum at reception. Headphones are run by cassette player or C.D. player or MP3 player, etc. All the information, related to the museum and its collection, are stored in it. When the visitor plays this device he can listen to all the information about the collection which he is looking at the moment.

Speakers are installed in the galleries to provide information about the collection of museum. This technique is very useful in natural history museums and ethnographic museums where with the help of this technique dramatic sound effect can be created to provide a unique atmosphere of jungle or village or some other planet. This technique is equally useful in museum of musical instruments where visitors can listen to the music of different musical instruments.

Gallery Talk

A lecture delivered in the gallery by an expert of that collection is known as gallery talk. The date and time of the gallery talk should be advertised some days before so that a lot of people may visit a gallery. Each and every aspect of the collection of that gallery is discussed in detail under a gallery talk. Here, visitors are free to ask any question related to the collection of that gallery.

Dioramas and Models

Dioramas and models are the communication tools of a museum which communicate to visitors about museum collection in a simple manner. Dioramas and models provide dramatic effect and create an atmosphere where a visitor can co-relate the objects with the situation. In other words, by the help of dioramas and models the museum object itself communicates to visitors.

Touch Screen Computers

Touch screen computers are installed in the gallery where a visitor-friendly software is installed with a good photograph and detailed information of all the exhibits. Any interested visitor can retrieve as much information as he can about a museum object. Visitors can easily understand the theme and history of collection with the help of these types of computers.

Museum Library

Museum collection communicates to people via library also. Museum library should be flooded with books relating to the nature of collection. Visitors, who are interested to know more about the museum collection, should be permitted to use the services of the library.

Museum Shop

Visitors can buy plaster casts, item of art and crafts, souvenirs, publications, CD, DVD, etc. from the museum shop. On the one hand, these articles provide various information about museum collection, on the other hand, these items keep alive memories of the museum visit for a long time and also encourage others to visit the museum.

Museum Communication Outside the Museum

It is a moral responsibility of a museum to communicate about its collection and provide its services to the people who do not come to the museum. There are so many ways of doing this :

(i) Press,

(ii) Radio,

(iii) Television,

(iv) Mobile Services,

(v) Website.

PRESS

Museums and press, by their mutual relationship, can play a very important role in creating an awareness among the masses. They both can complement each other. On the one hand press (newspapers, magazines, etc.) can get tons of information from museums and on the other hand, museums can present their collection with detailed information among the masses with the help of the press. All museums, no matter whether they are very big or too small, have some kind of news which can be used in the local press. News and feature stories about the museum's permanent collections, exhibitions, activities, new discoveries, educational and cultural programmes and news about special visitors are all usable by the press. Apart from this, with the help of press, museums can alert citizens through announcements of cultural and educational programmes, gallery talk, special lectures, film shows, seminars, concerts, etc. In case of any special event the museum should invite journalists and columnists to the museum so that they may write their views about the museum and publish it in their newspapers. Articles published in newspapers will have positive effect on people and provide them impetus to visit the museum.

RADIO

Radio is a powerful communication device which can be used by the museum for disseminating knowledge about their artefacts and other services to the people and motivate them to come to the museum. The museum can prepare a variety of programmes for radio which are usable for all radio, museum and people. Programmes can be recorded in the museum or in the studio of a radio station. Interview with the director or curator of the museum can be recorded and can be broadcast by the radio station. Programmes on open discussion can also be recorded in the studio of radio where topics on any newly arrived artefacts and new exhibitions organized by the museum can be discussed.

Sometimes radio correspondents, for covering the news, also visit the museum on special occasions like opening ceremony of a special exhibition, opening of any new gallery in the museum or any distinguished visitor visiting the museum, etc.

TELEVISION

Television is one of the strongest and most successful communication device which is highly beneficial for museums. Museum can prepare weekly, biweekly or daily programme on its artefacts, galleries or exhibitions for television. News related to the museum like new arrivals of objects, planning of a new exhibition, museum visited by any renowned visitor, etc., programmes on quiz, interviews, open discussions, discoveries and new findings of the museum, new research activities done by the museum, new publications of the museum, etc. can be prepared for television by museums. Documentary films, based on the collection of the museum or any civilization or ancient history of a particular city or site, can also be prepared by the museum.

MOBILE SERVICES

The main idea behind the mobile service is that if people do not come to see the museum then the museum itself should go near the people by its mobile service in the form of bus. This museum bus consists of plaster casts of original objects, maps, drawings, models, prints, participatory exhibits, etc. with proper lighting and information labels. Mobile service is used to attract people towards museum. Sometimes these mobile exhibitions are organized in trains also. When India was celebrating the 50th year of its Independence two trains, carrying photographs, paintings, sculptures, etc. related to India's cultural legacy, travelled all over India. One train travelled from north to south and other train travelled from east to west. These trains were halting at every stations for few days so that people may see the exhibition and understand such a rich cultural heritage of India.

WEBSITE

Website is a powerhouse of information technology. Unlimited information can be stored in a website. Every museum should create and have a website so that the museum may connect to the rest of the world by internet. Website can be developed by a software expert or programmer. Museum should try to provide all the necessary information, relevant data related to artefacts with good quality photographs, list of museum services, facilities provided to museum visitors, various activities done by the museum, new findings, discoveries and research done by the museum, list of museum publications, new artefacts or collection acquired by the museum, announcements of lectures, gallery talk, seminars, special film shows, summer programmes for children, workshops for teachers or children, study tour for teachers and children, etc. People can see the museum and its collections with all the related information on website itself. After creating a website, the museum should update it from time to time so that people may get latest and relevant information about the museum and its collections.

10

Museum Administration

MUSEUM administration plays a key role in proper day-to-day functioning of the museum. Behind every successful museum there is always a good administration.

Types of Museum according to the Administrative Set-up

According to administrative set-up, museums can be classified into following parts :

1. Government museums,
2. Semi-government/Autonomous museums,
3. University museums,
4. Private museums.

GOVERNMENT MUSEUMS

Government museums may again be classified into four parts:

A. National Museums,
B. Museums of National Importance,
C. State level/Regional Museums,
D. Local/District Museums,
E. Site Museums.

National Museums

National Museums are run by different ministries of Government of India. For example,

(i) National Museum of India, New Delhi (under Department of Culture).

(ii) National Gallery of Modern Art (under Department of Culture).

(iii) National Museum of Natural History (under Environment/Forest Ministry).

(iv) National Rail Museum (under Railway Ministry).

(v) National Museum of Handloom and Craft (under Ministry of Textile).

Museums of National Importance

After seeing the much diversified, big and prestigious collection Government of India has declared four museums as a "Museum of National Importance" namely:

(i) Allahabad Museum, Allahabad.

(ii) Indian Museum, Kolkata.

(iii) Prince of Wales Museum, Mumbai.

(iv) Salarjung Museum, Hyderabad.

State Level/Regional Museums

State/Regional museums are governed by the state government. State museums display the objects which belong to that particular state so that people may see the cultural heritage of that state. The example of state/regional museums is as follows :

(i) U.P. State Museum, Lucknow.
(ii) Bihar State Museum, Patna.
(iii) Assam State Museum, Guahati.
(iv) Karnataka State Museum, Bangalore.
(v) Rajasthan State Museum, Jaipur.
(vi) M.P. State Museum, Bhopal.

Local/District Museums

Local/District museums are governed by the Municipal corporations. The cultural heritage and the objects belonging to that particular district are kept for display. The examples of these kinds of museums are:

(i) Mathura Museum, Mathura.
(ii) Sarnath Museum, Sarnath.
(iii) Kaushambi Museum, Kaushambi.
(iv) Kurukshetra Museum, Kurukshetra.

Site Museums

Site museums are governed by the Archaeological Survey of India, which come under the Department of Culture. There are nearly 40 site museums in India. Site museum represents the objects for display which belong to that particular site only. The example of such types of museums are:

(i) Nagarjunikonda Museum, Nagarjunikonda.
(ii) St. George Museum, Chennai.
(iii) Purana Quila Museum, New Delhi.

(iv) Indian War Memorial Museum, Red Fort, New Delhi.

(v) Khajuraho Museum, Khajuraho.

(vi) Site Museum, Lothal.

Apart from these museums, seven zonal museums under the Anthropological Survey of India also come in this category.

SEMI-GOVERNMENT/AUTONOMOUS MUSEUMS

Semi-government/Autonomous museums are governed by a Trust or Society. A trust must be registered under "Trust Act, 1882" while a society should be registered under the "Society Registration Act, 1860." The overall administration of the society/trust can be divided into three phases:

(i) Board of Management,

(ii) Executive Committee, and

(iii) Finance Committee.

Board of Management

Board of management consists of all the trustees (in case of trust) or members (in case of society). The number of trustees or members may be approximately 10 to 15 or up to 20. These members are the policy makers and bear the overall responsibility of the museum-related work.

Executive Committee

The trust/society also has a small executive committee which consists of four to five members namely chairman, vice-chairman, general secretary, treasurer, director. It is not possible for the board to solve each and every issue in its meeting, so the executive committee is given the work to solve day-to-day problems and properly execute the policies made by the board.

Finance Committee

The finance committee is responsible for budget making and it also discusses income and expenditure plans for the museum. Normally the treasurer of the executive committee should be the chairman of the finance committee.

The best example of this type of museum is "International Roerich Memorial Trust," Kullu. This trust runs two museums. Chief Minister of Himachal Pradesh is the chairman of this trust. Another example is "Indian Archaeological Society," New Delhi which runs a museum "Indraprastha Museum of Art and Archaeology."

UNIVERSITY MUSEUMS

University museums are run by the university. Actually university departments run the museum to explain the subject better with visual knowledge to students. Some museums which are being run by the universities are as follows :

(i) Dr G.R. Sharma Memorial Museum (Dept. of Ancient Indian History, Culture & Archaeology, University of Allahabad).

(ii) Anthropology Museum (Dept. of Anthropology, University of Delhi).

(iii) Bharat Kala Bhawan (Banaras Hindu University).

(iv) Anatomy Museum (Madras Medical College).

(v) Anthropological Museum (Dept. Anthropology, Gauhati University).

(vi) Anthropological Museum (University of Ranchi).

(vii) Archaeological Museum (Dept. of Ancient History, Archaeology and Culture, Gorakhpur University).

(viii) Archaeological Museum (Dept. of Archaeology, Deccan College).

(ix) Asutosh Museum of Indian Art (University of Calcutta).

PRIVATE MUSEUMS

Private museums are not dependant on the government in financial matters. These museums have their own rules and regulations. These museums are sometimes run by trust or societies. The founder of such type of museum donates some amount in favour of the museum which is called "Foundation Fund." This foundation fund provides financial security to the museum. However, these museums often get grants from the government under the scheme "Promotion and Strengthening of Regional and Local Museums." Some example of such types of museums are:

(i) Kelkar Museum, Pune.

(ii) Shankar's International Dolls Museum, New Delhi.

(iii) Utencil Museum, Ahmedabad.

(iv) Calico Museum of Textile, Sarabhai Foundation, Ahmedabad.

11

Museum Infrastructure

At least three basic things (also called 3Ms) are necessary for museum infrastructure. These are man (staff), money (fund) and material (equipment).

Staff

Staff is a basic necessity for a museum. Museums having trained and educated staff get visitor's appreciation. The number of staff and their posts vary from museum to museum. But an ideal museum may have these kinds of posts:

1. Director.
2. Assistant Director.
3. (i) Curator (one for each section),
   (ii) Deputy Curator,
   (iii) Curatorial Associate,
   (iv) Clerk-cum-Computer Operator.
4. (i) Museum Education Officer,
   (ii) Senior Guide Lecturer,
   (iii) Guide Lecturer,
   (iv) Slide and Film Operator,
   (v) Museum Bus Driver,
   (vi) Museum Bus Cleaner.

5. (i) Museum Security Officer,
   (ii) Security Assistant,
   (iii) Gallery Attendant,
   (iv) Armed Guards,
   (v) Chowkidars,
   (vi) Sweepers.
6. (i) Publication Officer,
   (ii) Research Officer,
   (iii) Publication Assistant,
   (iv) D.T.P. Operator,
   (v) Draftsman,
   (vi) Publication Storekeeper.
7. (i) Exhibition Officer (Director, Exhibition),
   (ii) Assistant Director (Exhibition),
   (iii) Keeper (Exhibition),
   (iv) Deputy Keeper (Exhibition),
   (v) Marksman,
   (vi) Draftsman,
   (vii) Workshop Supervisor (carpentry),
   (viii) Carpenters,
   (ix) Assistant Carpenters,
   (x) Chief Electrician,
   (xi) Assistant Electrician,
   (xii) Generator Operator,
   (xiii) Chief Painter (Artist),
   (xiv) Assistant Painter,
   (xv) Bandhanis (skilled Labourers).

8. (i) Keeper (Modelling),
   (ii) Chief Modeller,
   (iii) Head Modeller,
   (iv) Modellers,
   (v) Moulders,
   (vi) Modelling Attendants.
9. (i) Chief Conservator,
   (ii) Assistant Conservator,
   (iii) Preservation Assistant,
   (iv) Laboratory Attendants.
10. (i) Administrative Officer,
   (ii) Junior Administrative Officer,
   (iii) Head Clerk,
   (iv) Accountant,
   (v) Cashier,
   (vi) Receptionist,
   (vii) Vendor (for museum shop),
   (viii) Chief Chef (for museum cafeteria),
   (ix) Assistant Chef,
   (x) Attendants,
   (xi) Ticket Seller,
   (xii) Ticket Checker.
11. (i) Store Officer (Store Keeper),
   (ii) Clerks,
   (iii) Typists.
12. (i) Librarian,

- (ii) Assistant Librarian,
- (iii) Library Attendants.

13. (i) Photo Officer,
    - (ii) Senior Photographer,
    - (iii) Assistant Photographer,
    - (iv) Attendants.

For filling such a variety of posts in a museum we really need a careful consideration. However, there are three ways by which a museum can employ suitable staff. These are:

1. Selection,
2. Promotion, and
3. Deputation.

SELECTION

Museums can recruit its staff by selection. Museum can take help from UPSC (Union Public Service Commission) or SSC (Staff Selection Commission) or any other agency in this regard. UPSC may provide Grade A and B staff to museum such as director, Assistant director, keepers, deputy keepers, etc., while SSC provides grade C and D staff to museum such as UDC, LDC, computer operators, accountants, typists, etc.

First of all, museum should tell these agencies about vacant posts, its minimum educational qualification, experience, essential and desirable qualifications. Thereafter these agencies start the selection process accordingly like publishing advertisement for filling up the vacant posts in different newspapers, conduct written examination (if necessary pre-examination, then main examination), interview, etc.

PROMOTION

Promotion is also a useful method of filling up a post. If one person retires or leaves a museum, then besides selecting a new candidate, a museum can deploy his junior to that post. For example, if a keeper retires, then his deputy (keeper) may be promoted to the post of keeper. However, it is necessary for the deputy to possess essential educational qualifications and experience.

DEPUTATION

Deputation is also a useful method of filling up a post temporarily. If one person goes abroad for two years for training, then there is an urgency to fill his post temporarily for two years, so that the functioning of the museum may not be affected. For this reason, a museum selects another museum's staff who carries essential educational qualifications and experience for the required post. Once his term completes, he goes back to his previous museum.

TRAINING

Time to time training for museum staff is very much essential for the smooth functioning of the museum. There can be two types of training for museum staff.

1. Pre-Service Training
2. In-Service Training

Pre-service training is provided to a person before joining a museum. The main aim behind this training is to apprise the employee of his nature of duties, his work profile and techniques of completing the task.

In-service training is provided to museum staff while they are in service. The basic aim of this training is to introduce the latest research and techniques to the museum employees.

Workshops, refresher courses, etc. are also examples, of this type of training. Different nature of work needs different type of training. For example, curators, conservators, employees of display section, security personnel, etc. need different kind of training. So, museums should arrange proper facilities of training to their staff from time to time.

Budget and Annual Action Plan

Planning a budget is an important work which is done by every museum. Planning of a budget starts one year before for the next financial year (April to March). Budget includes each and every expense the museum is going to incur during the next financial year. It includes salary of staff, electricity and water bill, telephone expenses, acquisition of artefacts, procurement of books for museum library, procurement of chemicals and instruments for conservation laboratory, procurement of paints, lights, bulbs, wood, etc. for display section, etc.

There are two types of budget:

1. Non-plan Budget, and
2. Plan Budget.

NON-PLAN BUDGET

The expenditure which happens every year is called non-plan budget. The example of this kind of budget is salary of museum staff, electricity/water expenses, office expenses (travel charges, stationery, etc.), and so on. These are the fixed expenditures which increase at certain rate annually. The budget planner must study this rate carefully and include it in the budget. For example, if there is an increment of 10 per cent in staff's salary then the budget planner should include the revised salary structure in the budget.

PLAN BUDGET

Plan budget is a budget which is prepared after a lot of consideration and planning. For example, the expenses on opening of a new museum gallery, publication of a revised museum catalogue, taking up of new museum projects, setting up a new temporary exhibition, etc. are included in a plan budget.

Annual Action Plan

Annual Action Plan is a detailed description of activities which a museum is planning for the next financial year. It also includes when the activities will start, when they will finish, and how much they will cost to the museum.

Annual Action Plan

Project	*April, May, June*	*July, Aug., Sept.*	*Oct., Nov., Dec.*	*Jan., Feb., March*	*Expenditure* (Rs.)
Setting up a temporary exhibition	Selection of objects	Mounting, framing & designing of an exhibition	Opening of an exhibition	On show	10 lakh
Publishing a catalogue	Selection of photos, collecting detailed descriptions, etc.	Sending matter to the press	Final proof-reading	Release	5 lakh
Workshop for school children	Preliminary preparation	Meeting with school principals and convince them to send children to museum for workshop	Workshop starts		3 lakh

Museum Equipments

Museum equipment play a vital role in the proper functioning of a museum. Museum equipment include lighting bulbs, furniture, fans, air-conditioners, stationery, computers, phones, fax, security devices (x-ray machines, metal detectors, CCTV, etc.), equipment related to the conservation laboratory, xerox machines, etc. Procuring, proper maintenance and proper upkeep of all these museum equipment need a lot of attention by museum authorities. Authorities, while procuring objects for museum, must keep the following things in their mind:

1. The quality of the object should be very good and its price should be very reasonable.
2. Guarantee of the object should be ensured. If anything happens to the object in guarantee period, the object should be replaced with a new one.
3. There must be an expert in a museum, who should give his opinion about the object, its authenticity and its usage.
4. After purchasing of an electronic/electrical item (like xerox machines, x-ray machines, CCTV, TV, DVD player, AC, fridge, etc.) proper training should be given to museum staff with a view to its handling, maintenance, proper servicing, etc. Proper handling and usage of the object enhance its longevity.

Methods of Acquiring Objects

There are five methods by which a museum can purchase its desired objects

1. Shopping from an open market,
2. Tender,
3. Global tender,

4. Specialized or unique items, and
5. Government agencies.

SHOPPING FROM AN OPEN MARKET

Shopping from an open market is a very easy and useful method of acquiring objects. For buying an object from an open market, museum authorities should consult at least 3-4 shops and check their quality and price. If the object seems suitable, then it may be acquired immediately.

TENDER

If museum wants to purchase many objects in quantities, then inviting tender is very much useful method of acquiring objects. An advertisement containing list of objects and its quantities should be published in different newspapers. In this advertisement, objects should be described in detail like which company's object museum wants, its size, type, etc. The closing date should also be mentioned here. After the last date of the tender, museum administration may open the sealed tenders in front of at least 2-3 top officers. Tender must be awarded to that firm which has quoted the lowest price.

GLOBAL TENDER

If any material is not available in the country but available outside then it may be procured through a global tender. The material coming in this category may include highly technical objects like air-conditioned showcases with all the necessary preservatives inside to prevent deterioration of museum artefacts, specialized lighting bulbs having no harmful rays, specialized chemicals for conservation laboratory, ultra modern security devices, etc. Such items come in this category. Advertisement may be given to different international newspapers and may be put in the websites in internet. Here also tender should be awarded to that firm which has quoted the lowest price. However, the matter regarding transportation, installation and proper training to the museum staff (like handling and proper upkeep of the object or machine) must be solved before.

SPECIALIZED OBJECTS

Sometimes only one company makes a specialized object. In this case museums have no alternative but to procure the same object. So, there is no need of a tender in this case. The object may be procured from the company directly. For example, only Philips company makes spot light bulbs in India, so museum can buy these bulbs from the company directly.

GOVERNMENT AGENCIES

Museums can also purchase their required goods from government agencies at reasonable prices. Super Bazar, DGS&D (Directorate General of Supplies and Disposals), Kendriya Bhandar, etc. are such government agencies from where small items (like pen, pencil, register, paper, etc.) as well as big items (computer, etc.) can be procured.

Stock Register

It is very necessary to maintain a record of every museum material or equipment. On the one hand, it provides proper security to museum objects against theft and misuse, and on the other hand, it also provides us prior information that such and such objects are about to finish. So the museum authorities may start the acquisition process accordingly in time. The total material of the museum can be divided into two parts:

1. Consumable material, and
2. Non-consumable material.

Consumable materials are such items as are used once and after some time are out of stock. Examples of consumable items are pen, pencil, paper, CDs, floppies, register, toner, bulbs, etc.

Non-consumable materials are such items as are used again and again for a long time. Examples of non-consumable items are fan, A.C., table, chair, xerox machines, computer, almirahs, etc.

Consumable material and non-consumable material both should be entered in stock register separately. Stock register keeps the record of mainly three things: how much material was received, to whom it is issued (quantity also) and after issuing the material how much it left.

Stock Register

Date	*Receipt*	*Issued to*	*Quantity*	*Sign*	*Balance*
1.4.09	200 Reams Paper	Mr. Atul Kumar	10 Ream	Sd/-	190 Ream
14.4.09	20 Computer cartridges	Mr. Alok Kishan	1 Cartridge	Sd/-	19 Cartridges
18.4.09	20 Toners	Mr. Avadh Bihari	1 Toner	Sd/-	19 Toners
25.4.09	50 CDs	Mr. Rajesh Kumar	5 CDs	Sd/-	45 CDs

Verification

Verification of museum materials and stock register is very essential from time to time. By verification the museum checks its materials and sees whether the material is being used properly or not. If someone is misusing the museum material, he may be caught by verification. Museum verification should be done by a highly placed museum officer or verification officer. After verifying the museum materials, the museum officer signs a "verification report." Museum officer also writes his comments on "verification report." If he finds any irregularities during verification, he should write about this in his "verification report."

Obsolete Materials

After verification if the verification officer finds some equipment/materials useless, he may declare them as obsolete materials. Obsolete materials may be a broken table, chairs, outdated computers, old newspapers/magazines, etc.

Auction

After declaring the museum equipment/materials obsolete, auction process starts. An advertisement is issued in different newspapers mentioning date and time of auction with a list of materials. On the fixed date and time people come for auction. Highest bidder takes away the desired object.

Audit

Every museum activity and programme for which money is spent by the museum is evaluated by audit. Auditor checks the museum record and finds out whether the money is properly utilized or not. Auditor also finds out whether the legal procedure was followed while acquiring museum equipment such as whether tender was issued, whether tender was given to the lowest bidder, whether the material which was acquired is of superior quality, whether the correct price was paid, etc. After the audit if the auditor is satisfied with all the museum expenditure, he issues an "utilization certificate" and gives his "Audit Report."

12

Museum Ethics

THE words "ethics" and "morality" are often interchangeable when it comes to conduct in public life. Both the words are valid terms referring to character and conduct of not only individuals but also institutions, groups of people and societies. The word "moral" is derived from the Latin word "Moralis," while "ethics" came from the Greek word "Ethos."

"Museum ethics" is all about the honesty, accountability, pursuit of excellence, loyalty, integrity of the people who man a museum, take all its decisions and then implement them with clear conscience so that it becomes collective in nature, hence institutional. Museum ethics, therefore, deals with value-judgments and the process of decision-making. Museum ethics is about how people and objects are treated in a museum. Most museum professionals have been feeling the need for a code of ethics for establishing basic standards for decision-making by which they could act and be evaluated. Museum ethics is related to all the branches and all the works of museum, hence comprehensive. The aim of the ethics is not only to differentiate between the right and wrong things to do in a museum but also to provide an accepted reference.

A museum anywhere in the world is expected to work according to international norms prescribed from time to time by international bodies of professional museologists. For example, it should acquire its objects according to its own collection-policy which is determined by its scope. It is the responsibility of the museum administration to use the collection for the creation and dissemination of knowledge through research, educational work, permanent display, temporary exhibitions, and other special activities and publications on them.

Museum authority should take special care while acquiring the museum objects. These must be genuine and not fake. These should be acquired only from authentic sources. Illegal trade of antiquities should not be encouraged by the museum whatever may be the lure.

Museum professionals should be very careful while de-accessioning the objects in its collection which some museums do from time to time. It should be done only if the object is totally damaged or badly deteriorated ruling out restoration. One of the essential obligations of each member of the museum profession is to ensure the proper care and conservation of both existing and newly-acquired objects for its collection. Museum collection should be secure for future generations.

The arrangement of proper training of museum professionals, in which museum ethics also finds a place, should be made by the museum authorities. Museum official should be told to strictly avoid unprofessional, that is unethical conduct whatever may be the cost. In particular, no museum official should accept any gift, hospitality, or any form of reward from any dealer, auctioneer or other persons whose interests are not above board since these may become improper inducements in respect of the purchase or disposal of museum items.

13

Conservation of Museum Objects

DECAY is a natural process. Every man-made creation also faces it at some point of time in its life. But by the help of conservation techniques this decay in museum objects can be restricted for a long period of time. There are three major factors that cause threat to the objects in the museum. These are Light, Humidity and Biological agents.

Light

Light is a form of energy which runs in the form of waves. The highest point of this wave is called "crest" while the lowest point is called "trough." The distance between 2 crests or 2 troughs is called "wavelength." The rays of light are of seven types: Gamma rays, X-rays, Ultraviolet rays, Visible rays, Infrared rays, Microwave, Radio wave. Radio wave has much less energy but it has the longest wavelength while gamma rays have very much energy and it has shortest wavelength.

Human eyes can see only visible rays. There are seven kinds of visible rays. These are violet, indigo, blue, green, yellow, orange, and red. Beyond the colour violet, ultraviolet rays start which are very dangerous to the art objects and which start ultraviolet radiation. A few points are being written here to avoid ultraviolet radiation on artefacts:

1. There must be a sufficient distance between the object and the light.
2. There are in the market two kinds of artificial lighting — "incandescent lamp" and "fluorescent tube." Incandescent lamp has very less ultraviolet radiation but it produces much heat which is also harmful to organic exhibits. The best method of lighting in a museum is the fluorescent tubes of cool type. The Philips 37 fluorescent tube has very low ultraviolet rays which is most suitable for a museum. But since it produces flat light, it does not highlight exhibits or their parts, like jewellery gems.
3. Ideally, the light should be covered by ultraviolet filters.
4. The glass panes of the showcases and the wall should be coated with titanium oxide or zinc oxide which absorbs ultraviolet rays.
5. We can measure ultraviolet radiation by the instrument called "UV Monitor." Microwatt per Lumen (µwatt/lumen) is the measuring unit of ultra-violet radiation. The UV radiation must be below 50 micro watt per lumen in a museum to avoid deterioration in exhibits.
6. Lux is a measuring unit of light. 10 lux is equal to 1 foot-candle light. Textiles, manuscripts, miniature paintings, natural history objects, etc. are to be displayed in not more than 50 lux to save them from the harmful rays of light. Horn, bones, ivory, oil

paintings, etc. should be displayed in not more than 150 lux otherwise the organic ingredients of these objects will get destroyed very soon. But metal objects, stone objects, glass, jewellery can be displayed in 1000 lux since these are non-organic materials.

Humidity

Humidity is the amount of water vapour in air. "Relative humidity" or "RH" is defined as "the ratio of the partial pressure of water vapour in a gaseous mixture of air" and "water vapour to the saturated vapour-pressure of water at a given temperature." Relative humidity is expressed as a percentage. The relative humidity should remain between 45 per cent and 60 per cent in a museum. We can measure the humidity by the instruments called Thermohygrograph and Whirling Hygrometer. A few points are mentioned here to control humidity in a museum:

1. If possible, museum should always use air-conditioning to maintain humidity level constant.
2. If A.C. is not possible, coolers, wet khas-khas curtains, can be used on windows and doors to increase humidity in the hot dry seasons of the region.
3. By the help of putting small plants in wet clay in a gallery we can increase humidity.
4. Silica gel, unslaked lime, calcium chloride, calcium oxide, thimobenzine can be used to decrease the humidity level in a museum because these materials absorb humidity or water vapour in the air.

Biological agents

Biological agents that cause damage to the museum objects can be divided into two parts: botanical agents like bacteria, algae, fungus, lichen, etc. and zoological agents like termite, silverfish, insect, pest, cockroach, rat, etc. A few points are mentioned here to control the attack of biological agents to the artefacts in a museum:

1. Every museum should have a conservation laboratory with at least the basic equipment and chemicals.
2. Small museums, which cannot afford such a laboratory, should make arrangements for a conservator's visit from time to time. If the object is found damaged then it must be sent immediately to the laboratory like National Museum Laboratory, National Research Laboratory for Conservation (NRLC) Lucknow, Indian National Trust for Art and Cultural Heritage (INTACH) New Delhi, etc. for conservation.
3. With the help of controlling and maintaining temperature (22° C) and relative humidity (45 to 60 per cent) the museum can control the intrusion of biological agents.
4. 10 per cent thymol solution is enough for preventing fungus growth in artefacts.
5. If the object is affected by insect or pest then it should be kept in the "Fumigation Chamber" which can be built in museums cheaply. In the chamber, which

could be a wooden almirah, certain chemicals should be kept for a certain period of time. These chemicals can be paradiclorobenzene, carbon disulphate, carbon tetrachloride, methyl bromide, ethylene oxide, carbonic sulphate, pentachlorophenol, thimole, etc. Their vapour kills silverfish, etc.

6. Barium carbonate is used to prevent rats in a museum.
7. Naphthalene balls should be kept besides the artefacts which prevent insect growth.
8. Cloroden, D.D.T., sodium floride, and baygon spray should be used to prevent cockroaches in a museum.

Conservation Techniques

In the museum, each category of artefacts needs treatment of conservation specific to the material; thus stone objects are treated differently from paper. Similarly, bronze is not treated the same way as the palm-leaf manuscripts. A brief conservation guideline is given below for conservation of museum artefacts.

STONE

Stone is a composite material of various minerals cemented together with argileous materials like clay and silt, etc. It is more stable than metal. Stones are affected by moss, lichen and algae appearing green in moist condition but after drying they appear black. The black deposit can be removed by the application of 10 per cent ammonia solution followed by careful brushing and washing.

The main cause of damage to stone objects is the presence of salts in them, which often appear on the surface of stone in the form of white efflorescence or powdery substance. The best method for curing the salt-laden stone objects is to treat them with the paper-pulp method. In this method, paper-pulp is soaked overnight in water and then applied all over the object in comparatively thick consistency, and allowed to dry. While the pulp is drying, it draws out the salts present in the stone. When the pulp is completely dry, it is removed from the object and thrown away. A test of Silver Nitrate or Barium Chloride is conducted to ascertain whether the salts are removed or not. If the salt is still present, the process is repeated till the salts are completely removed. After complete removal of the salts, the stone object is coated with a 2 per cent solution of polyvinyl acetate or acetone.

PALM-LEAF MANUSCRIPTS

Palm-leaves are one of the writing materials in India and the Far East. Grown palm-leaves were cut, dried, boiled in turmeric solution and punched, or else incised, to write letters or make images with the help of a stylus, a sharp nail or else nail-like object with knife edge. The leaves were cut to size, according to need.

The palm-leaf manuscripts are normally affected by insects tunnels are made by them across the leaf. At times the leaves are found stuck together. Stuck leaves are kept in a steam bath, after which they are easily separated. The leaves are cleaned with a 2 per cent solution of citronella oil or camphor oil. By applying this solution, the hardened leaves get softened, and flexibility is also restored. The insects are driven off by the oil, and the black colour adds visibility to the incised or stencilled matter.

CERAMICS

Ceramic is the general term used for an object made out of clay, like pottery, porcelain and earthenware. Clay was certainly among man's earliest discoveries for his needs. There are many types of firing of clay materials, such as "open firing," "closed firing" and "inverted firing." Normally fired clay will appear red when fired in a kiln with holes allowing oxygen to pass, and black when the kiln is completely closed but smoke and heat and not the fire bake the pottery. In the inverted firing, pots are kept in the kiln upside down with the result it is partly red and partly black. Unless the potteries are glazed or highly burnished they cannot be used to keep liquids. Therefore glazing is done after white clay vessels are fired by coating a paste containing the minerals of desired colours to colour the finished goods. This practice was in vogue during the Mogul rule in India. The East India Company in India too prepared ceramic vessels. However, it was in vogue during the Harappan times as well as in the Kushana period. The so-called "Muslim Glazed Wares" from Iran and Iraq came to India in the eighth-ninth centuries. Then the Chinese brought them, including porcelain to India.

The ceramic should be cleaned with water. The broken edges of ceramics are mended with *quickfix*, an adhesive which sets quickly. The broken and lost portions are reconstructed with the help of white *M-Seal*. A support is provided to reach the proper positioning of the mended portions. Terracotta and other baked clay objects, even those glazed, recovered from the earth during excavation are likely to contain salts which can be cleaned by leaching, i.e. soaked in clean plain water and then thoroughly cleaning softly in running water. After drying up, 5 per cent polyvinyl acetate is coated as a preserving coat.

BRONZE

Bronze is an alloy of copper and tin or copper and arsenic. It is called as *panchaloha* also as it is believed to be an alloy of five metals — copper, tin, gold, silver and lead. But mostly gold and silver are absent. If the environment is bad due to moist conditions, different corrosion products are formed. The corrosion products affect bronzes. A uniform thin green natural coating of basic copper carbonate is, of course, aesthetic to look at. It is also protective in nature. It is called *patina* which means "weathering from within" which is a time-taking natural process. When the corrosion product is copper chloride, it is unsightly like pimples on face and also powdery. It is called *bronze disease.* The bronze disease spreads from one place of the object to the other. The chloride is removed physically and stabilised by a 2 per cent solution of benzo-tri-azole. By this method the corrosion is arrested. A coating of 2 per cent poly vinyl acetate in acetone is given as a protective coating.

SILVER OBJECTS/COINS

Silver is a white metal, which turns black (silver sulphide) and white (silver chloride). The blackening of silver is called *tarnishing*. Silver objects/coins are cleaned by keeping them in a 10 per cent solution of formic acid to remove the black colour (silver sulphide) and immersed in a solution of 10 per cent ammonia to remove the white colour (silver chloride). After thorough washing, the coins are dried and coated with a 2 per cent solution of polyvinyl acetate in acetone as a preservative coating.

COPPER OBJECTS/COINS

Copper, and its alloys like bronze or brass, corrode easily, especially when buried in the earth with moisture. The soil contains much salt which changes the metal into its various salts. Corrosive layers of chloride cover the copper surface, rendering the metal fragile and weak. These corrosive layers with chloride in them have the capacity to continue converting fresh metal into salt, even after it is no longer in contact with the soil. This continued corrosion of copper is popularly referred to as "bronze disease." High humidity accelerates the development of bronze disease. These are cleaned with an alkaline solution of Rochelle salt (15 gms of Rochelle salt + 5 gms of sodium hydroxide + 80 gms of water). When the corrosion products are removed, the copper objects/coins appear red. The red cupric oxide corrosion is removed by soaking the coins in 10 per cent citric acid, washed well to remove the salts, dried and a preservative coating of 2 per cent polyvinyl acetate in acetone is provided.

PAINTING ON LEATHER

Art on leather originated from Persia. Illustrated

manuscripts were bound with richly decorated leather covers. These covers were either painted with miniatures or leather tooled and embossed with gold. Miniature paintings on leather are also found in the form of royal playing cards. The themes of these cards were primarily based on Hindu mythology. The processed leather is used as a support for paintings. A ground is prepared by priming the leather. The subject is drawn and natural colour pigments applied. Varnish is applied as a protective coating. Leather being organic in nature, it easily deteriorates. High humidity encourages the growth of micro-organisms, insects and pests. Dryness leads to brittleness, wrinkling and hardening of the leather. Dust, grease and dirt obscure the painting. Natural pollutants like oxides of sulphur, carbon, nitrogen, etc. dissolve in the moisture present in the atmosphere, resulting in acidity to the leather. To treat hardened, brittle leather, leather-dressing materials like castor oil, lemon grass oil or citronella oil is used. This restores flexibility. 0.1 per cent of chlorophenol is added as fungicide. Wrinkles may be removed by placing the leather under a weight press. Glycerin and rectified spirit are also used to flatten cupped leather with uneven surface. Fumigation with thymol and para-dichloro-benzene are required for prevention of insect and fungal attack.

OIL PAINTING ON CANVAS

The art of painting on canvas was introduced to India from the West. The cotton or linen canvas is normally the support. The support is made as a ground for the painting by the application of primers like lead oxide, zinc oxide, and titanium oxide. After drying, the surface is smoothened with a polisher of agate like semi precious stone. After that the painting is executed. In order to keep the pigments protected, a varnish coating is provided. Generally, the defects can be in any layer, viz. support, ground, pigment and varnish. The aged varnish layer, which masks the painting, may be removed by dissolution using rectified spirit as solvent and turpentine as the restrainer. The removal of the varnish layer makes the painting look fresh. Relining, using fresh seasoned canvas, and a suitable and reversible adhesive like mastic resin-wax mixture, can strengthen the weakened canvas. The loss of pigments may be restored using fresh pigments by a method called "infilling" followed by "retouching" by brush to match, by and large, the original.

WOOD

Wood, being an organic material, is especially susceptible to deterioration and great care is required for its preservation. We find various kinds of wooden artefacts in art museums, crafts museums, and ethnographical museums. If wood remains in a too humid and stagnant atmosphere for a long time, it may develop fungal growth which weakens the surface. A really dangerous type of fungal attack on wood is called "dry rot." Wood affected by this fungus becomes soft, spongy and light. To prevent this fungal growth, the affected object may be dried out in a shade. Application of 1 per cent solution of orthophenyl phenol in ethyl alcohol to the wooden object helps prevent the growth of fungus. Fumigation with a mixture of carbon disulphide in one part and carbon tetrachloride in four parts may be done for conserving wooden object from insects.

TEXTILES

Textiles are woven out of natural and synthetic fibres. The designs are created by weaving, dyeing, printing or painting. The dyes may be natural (mineral or organic dyes) and man-made synthetic materials. The ancient textiles had only natural dyes. Textiles are normally affected by moisture, biological agents, mishandling, vandalism, stains, etc. The tears are mended by darning if the textile is in fairly good condition and the fibres are strong. In case the fibres are weak, the textile should be lined with similar cloth and stitched with weak thread. Very fragile textile may be mended with similar cloth and pasted with the help of 20 per cent solution of polyvinyl acetate in acetone and pressed. Sometimes old textiles are lined with similar cloth and stitching with weak threads to avoid tear in the textile.

There are a hundred other kinds of materials out of which human beings made artefacts which find their way to museums. Bone, ivory, shell, clay, glass, iron, lead, silk, wool, etc. are only a few of them. Hence this list is only indicative and not exhaustive. It is essential that museums will have highly trained conservators in their laboratories since conservation of cultural property should not be attempted by untrained persons — it may do more harm to the objects than good if wrongly handled.

Setting up of Conservation Laboratory in a small Museum

A museum must have a conservation laboratory with all

the needed equipment. A list of some important equipment is being given below —

1. Thermometer
2. Whirling Hygrometer
3. Thermohygrograph
4. Microscope
5. Luxmeter
6. Spatula
7. Lamination Machine
8. Fumigation Chamber
9. Preservatives such as paradiclorobenzene, carbon disulphate, carbon tetrachloride, polyvinyl acetate, methyl bromide, ethylene oxide, carbonic sulphate, pentachlorophenol, thimole, silica gel, D.D.T., naphthalene, etc.
10. Different sizes of needles and threads
11. Different sizes of brushes
12. Medicated tissue papers
13. Litmus papers (blue and red)
14. pH papers

14

International Organizations
Conventions for Collection and Preservation of Antiquarian Remains

International Council of Museums (ICOM)

ICOM is the international organization of museums and museum professionals which is committed to the conservation, continuation and communication to the society of the world's natural and cultural heritage, present and future, tangible and intangible. It was created in 1946. ICOM is a non-governmental organization (NGO) maintaining formal relations with UNESCO and having a consultative status with the United Nations' Economic and Social Council. As a not-for-profit organization, ICOM is financed primarily by membership fees and supported by various governmental and non-governmental bodies. It carries out part of UNESCO's programme for museums. Its headquarters is located in Paris (France). The ICOM's Secretariat is housed in the UNESCO building in Paris. Under the direction of the Secretary General, the Secretariat is responsible for implementing the Executive Council's decisions. The Secretariat provides services to ICOM members. It co-ordinates the activities of committees, helps carry out its programmes and organizes meetings and assemblies for its directing bodies. The 21,000 members of ICOM in 140 countries participate in the national, regional and international activities of the organization: workshops, publications, training, twinning programmes, and the promotion of museums through International Museum Day (18 May annually).

ICOM's activities respond to the challenges and needs of the museum profession and are focused on the following themes:

- professional co-operation and exchange
- dissemination of knowledge and raising public awareness of museums
- training of personnel
- advancement of professional standards
- elaboration and promotion of professional ethics
- preservation of heritage and combating the illicit traffic in cultural property

International Centre for the Study of the Preservation and Restoration of Cultural Property (ICCROM)

The International Centre for the Study of the Preservation and the Restoration of Cultural Property (ICCROM) is an international, inter-governmental organization established in 1959. Created by UNESCO, ICCROM is an independent body currently consisting of 101 member nations and various associate institutions. With headquarters in the Ospizio di San Michele, Rome, it serves as a research and training centre and as a clearing house for the exchange of conservation information among specialists from all nations.

Concerned with the scientific and technical problems of cultural conservation, ICCROM collects and circulates information, institutes and co-ordinates research, and assists in training researchers and technicians and in raising the standard of restoration work. ICCROM has established itself as a leading international preservation institution.

In fulfilling its responsibilities to assist in training research workers and technicians, ICCROM offers a wide range of training courses at its headquarters in Rome and elsewhere. These courses focus on the conservation of sites, buildings, and artefacts of cultural and historical importance. Course participants, who include architects, urban planners, archaeologists, art historians, engineers, conservators, scientists, archivists, librarians, and museum curators, are carefully selected so that they are actively engaged in conservation work and training in their own countries whenever possible.

International Council on Monuments and Sites (ICOMOS)

It is an association of professionals throughout the world that currently bring together over 7,500 members. ICOMOS works for the conservation and protection of cultural heritage and places of antiquarian remains. It is the only global non-governmental organization of its kind, which is dedicated to promoting the application of theory, methodology, and scientific techniques to the conservation of the architectural and archaeological heritage. ICOMOS is a network of experts that benefits from the interdisciplinary exchange of its members, among which are architects, historians, archaeologists, art historians, geographers, anthropologists, engineers and town planners.

Some of its objectives are as follows —

- To bring together conservation specialists from all over the world and serve as a forum for professional dialogue and exchange;
- To collect, evaluate and disseminate information on conservation principles, techniques and policies;
- To co-operate with national and international authorities on the establishment of documentation centres specializing in conservation;
- To work for the adoption and implementation of international conventions on the conservation and enhancement of architectural heritage;
- To participate in the organization of training programmes for conservation specialists on a worldwide scale; and
- To put expertise of highly qualified professionals and specialists at the service of the international community.

World Federation of Friends of Museums (WFFM)

It is an international non-profit, non-governmental organization that unites and supports all friends of museums around the world. It was legally constituted in Belgium in 1975. WFFM brings together a growing number of friends and volunteers from all over the world, who understand the importance of combining their efforts in the conservation of humankind's cultural heritage.

The aim of the WFFM is to promote and spread the idea of Friends of Museums worldwide. The enrichment of museums and the safeguard of our cultural heritage are central to all the activities carried out by the Federation.

WFFM is an international organization that represents two million individual Friends of Museums, grouped in national federations as well as in numerous single associations throughout the world. WFFM considers that it is through the open and active participation of the community that museums will fully accomplish their mission.

WFFM's activities are as follows:

- To unite the growing number of Friends of Museums in different countries so as to facilitate the exchange of ideas and experiences in the conservation of cultural heritage;
- To promote the establishment and development of national federations and associations of Friends of Museums around the world, and support their initiatives towards the enrichment of museums;
- To foster the highest ethical standards amongst Friends and Volunteers of Museums using the precepts of the WFFM Code of Ethics;
- To communicate the idea and vision of Friends of Museums worldwide;
- To encourage ties between museum professionals and volunteers, young people and the general public;
- To officially represent the Friends of Museums in developing cultural co-operation with similar

international organizations, particularly with ICOM and UNESCO; and

- To generate public and government awareness of museums worldwide.

United Nations Educational, Scientific and Cultural Organization (UNESCO)

It was founded on 16 November 1945. Once a year, its World Heritage Committee meets to decide on additions to the World Heritage List, which includes the most outstanding cultural and natural sites around the globe. Inscription on this list is just the first step towards safeguarding these sites: management and preservation are ongoing processes, involving local communities as well as national authorities. So far, 183 countries have demonstrated their commitment to protecting our shared heritage by ratifying the World Heritage Convention.

UNESCO Convention on the Means of Prohibiting and Preventing the Illicit Import, Export and Transfer of Ownership of Cultural Property

(Paris, 14 November 1970)

The world's cultural heritage must be preserved and transferred to future generations. However, our cultural heritage is threatened every day; the pillage of archaeological sites and the theft of objects from museums are increasing on an unprecedented scale. Now, no country is free from this danger.

The 1970 UNESCO Convention declares as illegal the import, export or transfer of ownership of cultural property. By ratifying this Convention, each State Party undertakes to adopt the necessary measures:

(a) To prevent museums within their territories from acquiring cultural property which has been illegally exported;

(b) To prohibit the import of cultural property stolen from a museum or a public institution after the entry into force of the Convention; and

(c) At the request of the State of origin, to recover and return any such cultural property stolen and imported.

UNIDROIT Convention on Stolen or Illegally Exported Cultural Objects

(Rome, 24 June 1995)

The UNIDROIT (International Institute for Unification of Private Law) Convention on Stolen or Illegally Exported Cultural Objects is a complement to the UNESCO Convention. Perhaps the most important clause in the Convention is the principle that anyone with a stolen item in his/her possession must in all cases restore it. This rule forces buyers to check that the goods have come onto the market legally; otherwise they will have to be returned.

The UNESCO Convention of 1970 and the UNIDROIT Convention enable the preservation of cultural heritage and consequently the memory of humankind. They are a potent weapon in the fight against illicit traffic.

The ICOM Code of Professional Ethics

The ICOM Code of Professional Ethics was adopted unanimously by the 15th General Assembly of ICOM in Buenos Aires (Argentina), on 4 November 1986. It was amended by the 20th General Assembly in Barcelona (Spain) on 6 July 2001, retitled ICOM Code of Ethics for Museums, and revised by the 21st General Assembly in Seoul (Republic of Korea) on 8 October 2004. The ethics cover the following topics in detail —

1. Museums preserve, interpret and promote aspects of the natural and cultural inheritance of humanity;
2. Museums that maintain collections hold them in trust for the benefit of society and its development;
3. Museums hold primary evidence for establishing and furthering knowledge;
4. Museums provide opportunities for the appreciation, enjoyment, understanding and management of the natural and cultural heritage;
5. Museum hold resources that provide opportunities for other public services and benefits;
6. Museums work in close collaboration with the communities from which their collections originate as well as those they serve;
7. Museums operate in a legal manner; and
8. Museums operate in a professional manner.

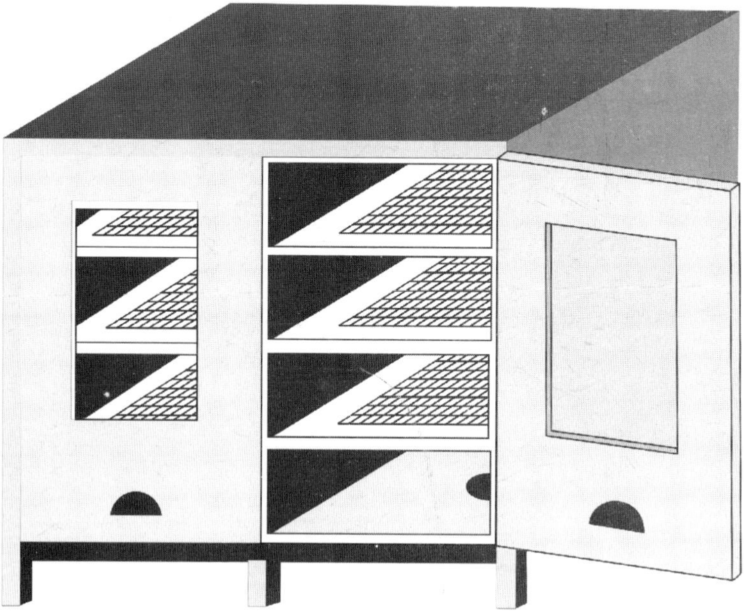

fig. 1. Fumigation chamber

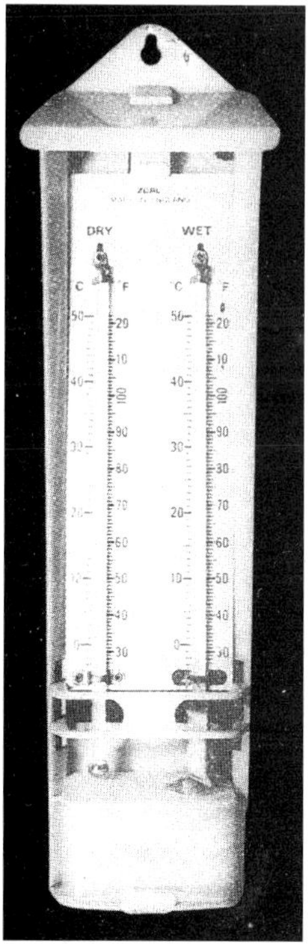

fig. 2. Thermometer

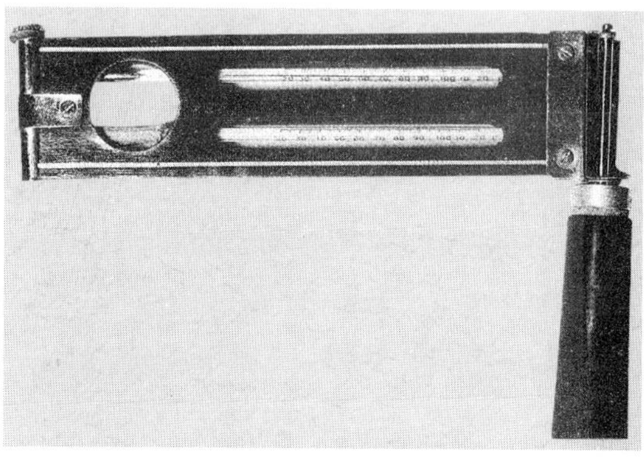

fig. 3. Whirling Hygrometer

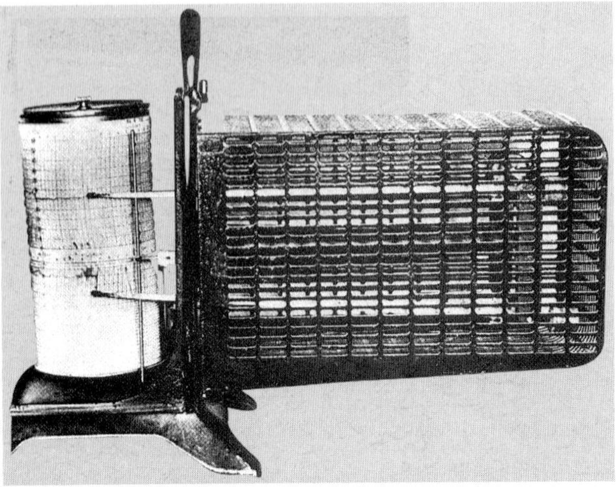

fig. 4. Thermohygrograph

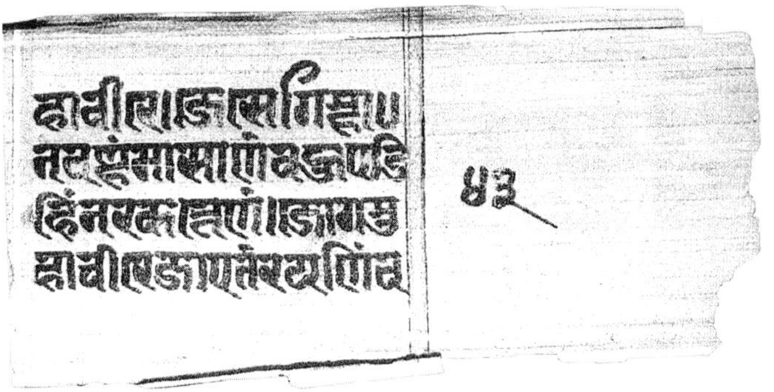

fig. 5. Palm-leaf Manuscript

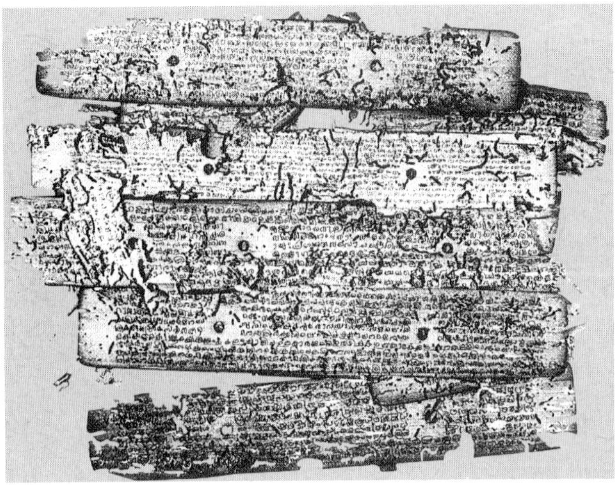

fig. 6. Damaged palm-leaf manuscript

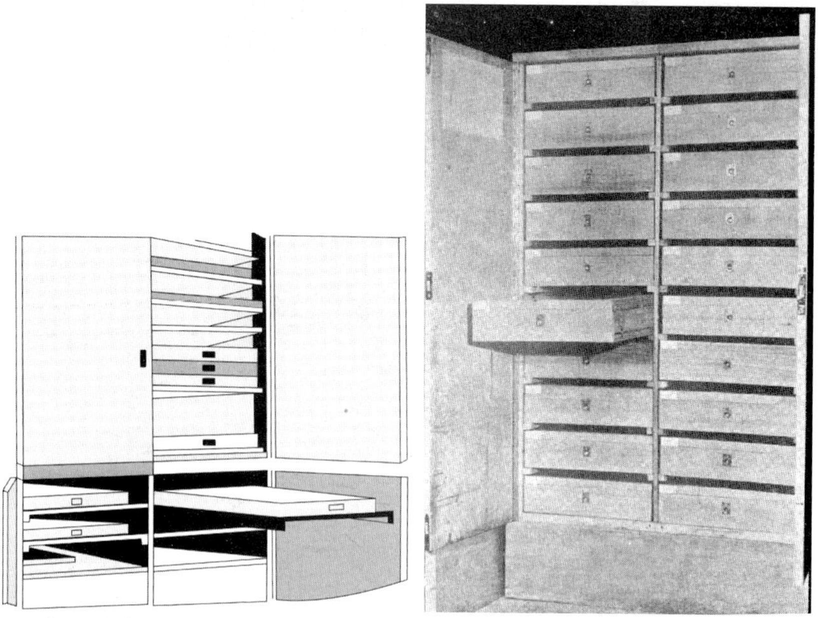

fig. 7. Cabinet of the store boxes containing paintings, manuscripts, etc.

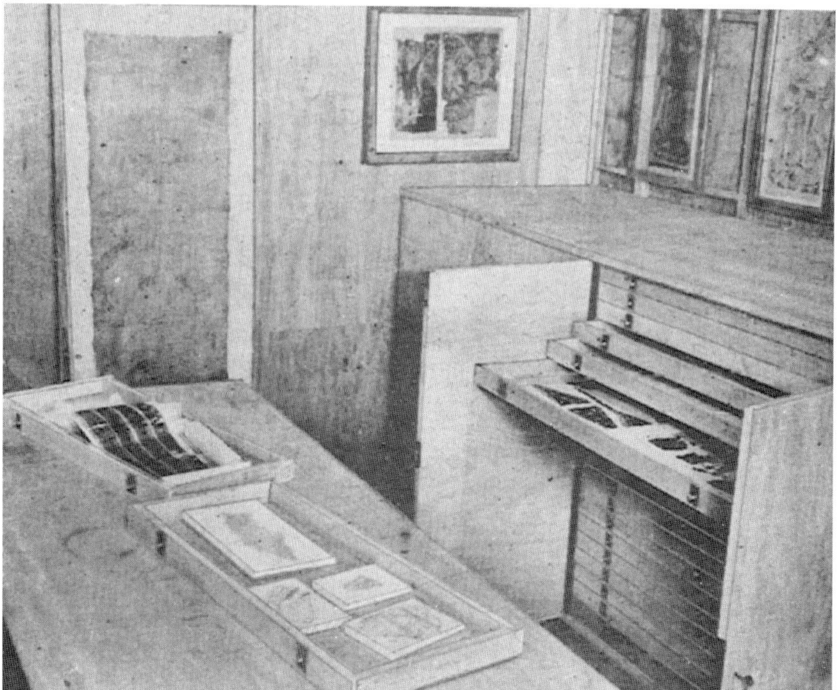

fig. 8. Storage furniture for paintings, etc.

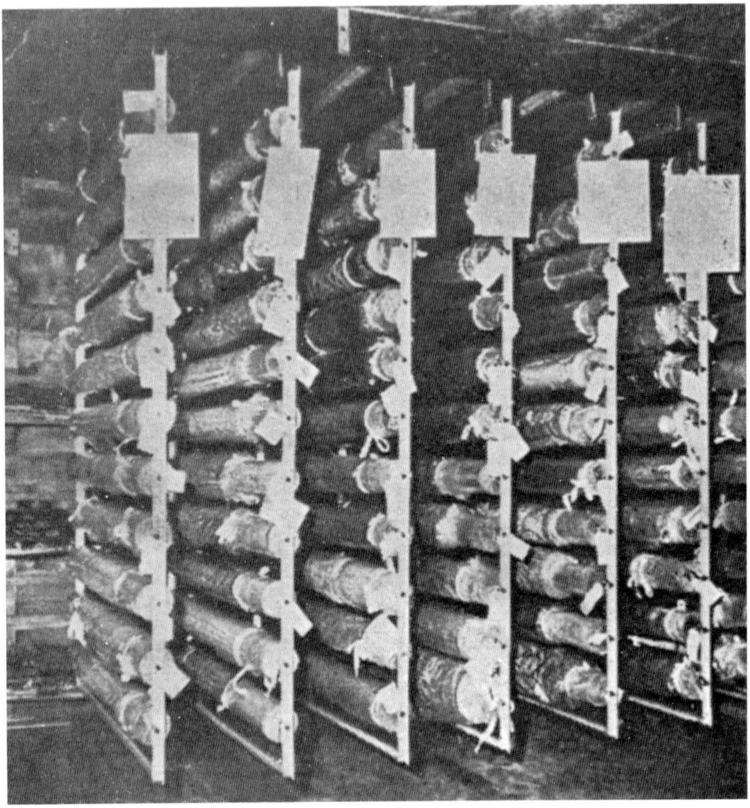

fig. 9. A gereral view of textile storage

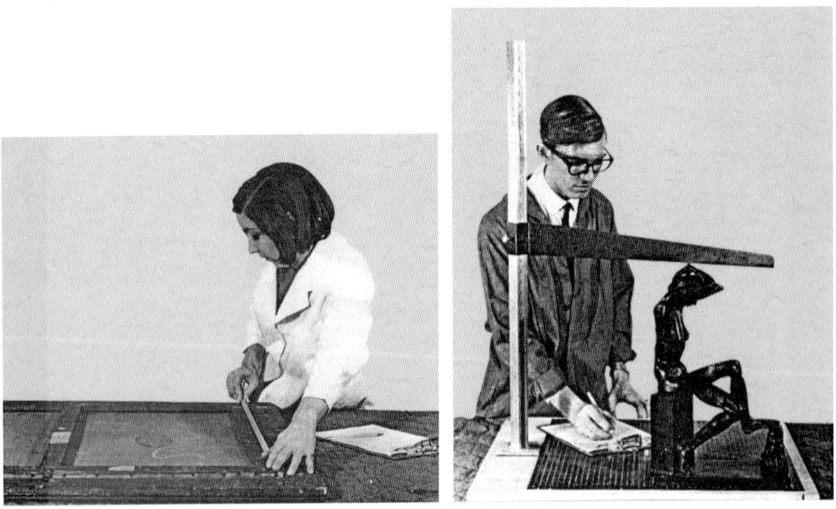

fig. 10 (a & b). Documentation work is being done by Museum Curators

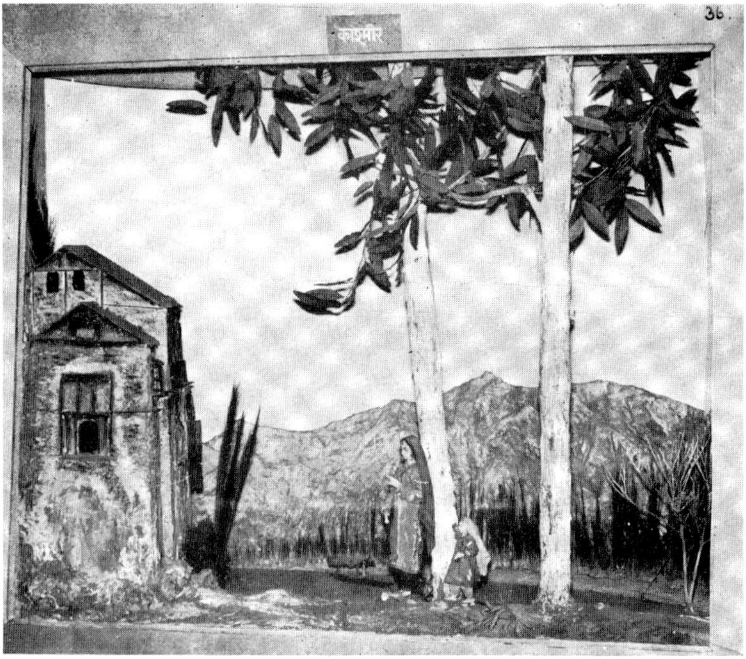

fig. 11. A Diorama showing the residents of Kashmir in their natural surroundings

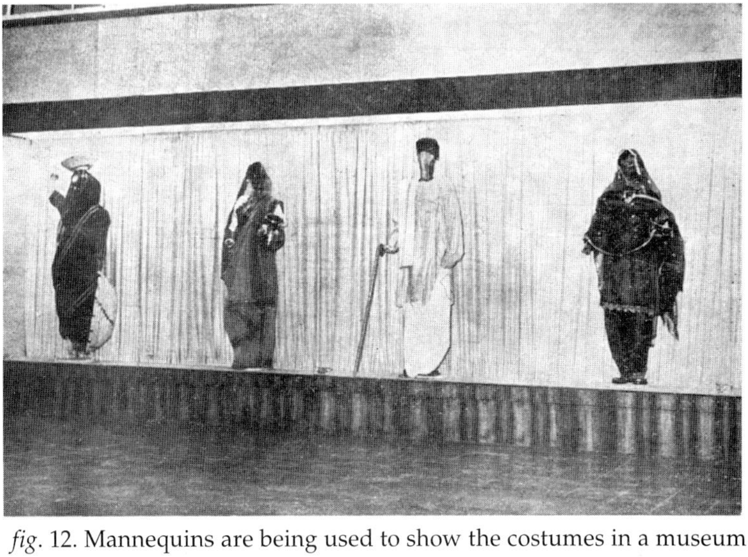

fig. 12. Mannequins are being used to show the costumes in a museum

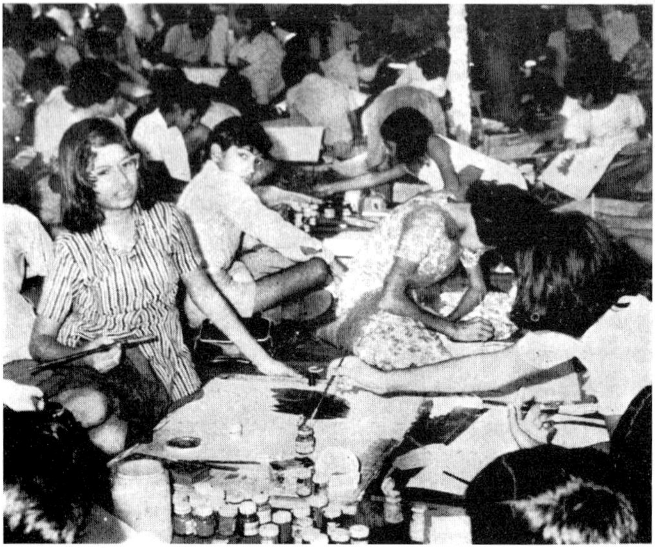

fig. 13. Children are participating in the painting competition

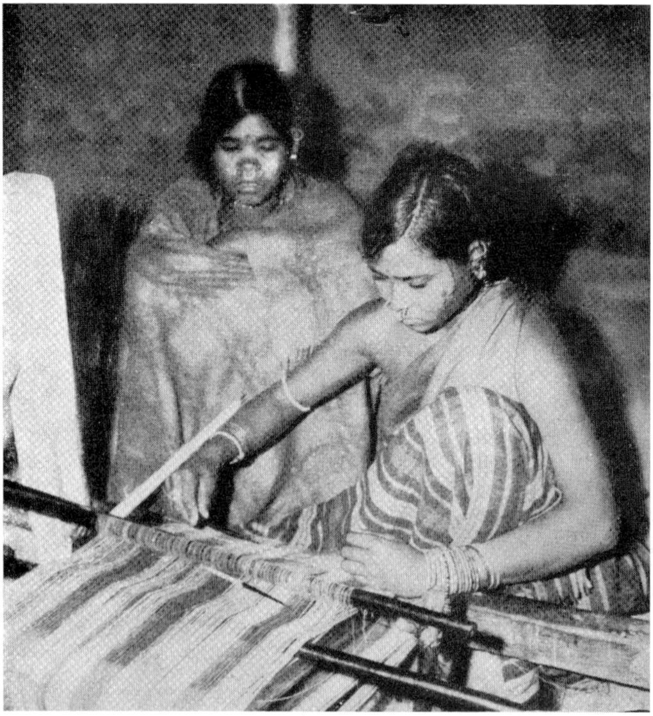

fig. 14. Women demonstrating live craft work in a Crafts Museum

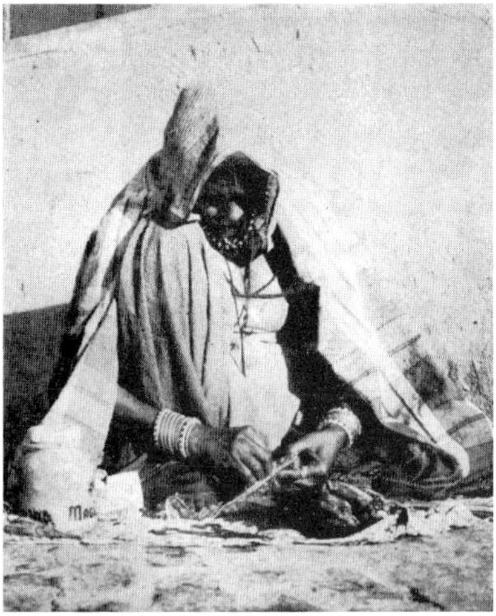

fig. 15. A woman giving demonstration on doll-making in Crarts Museum

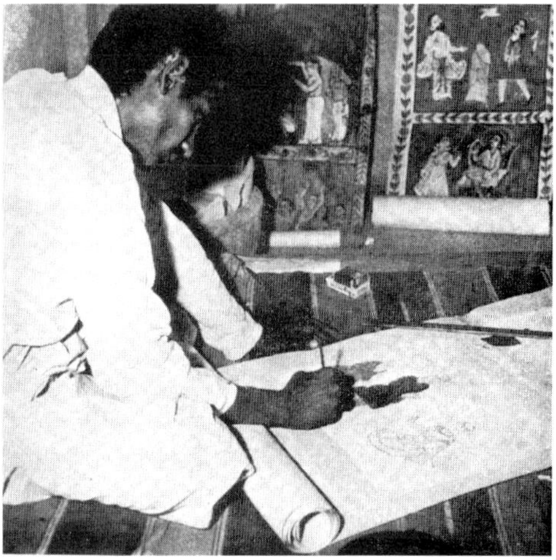

fig. 16. A man demonstrating Pata-chitra (scroll-painting) making in Crafts Museum

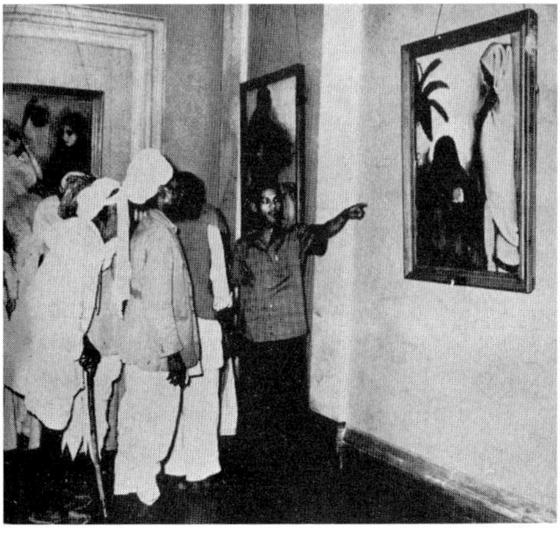

fig. 17. A guided tour is being conducted in the National Gallery of Modern Art

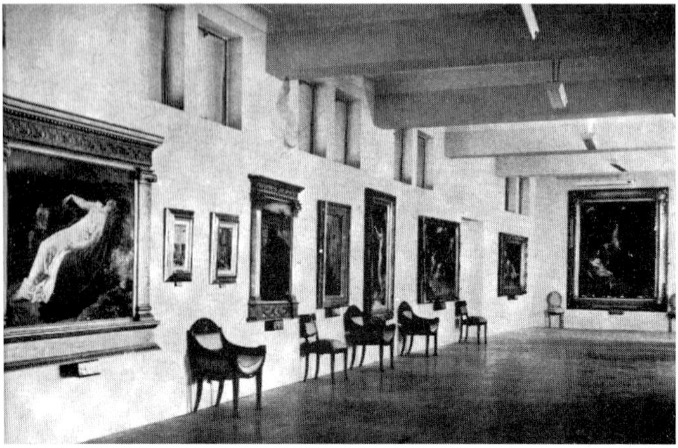

fig. 18. A view of the Painting Gallery in Salarjung Museum, Hyderabad

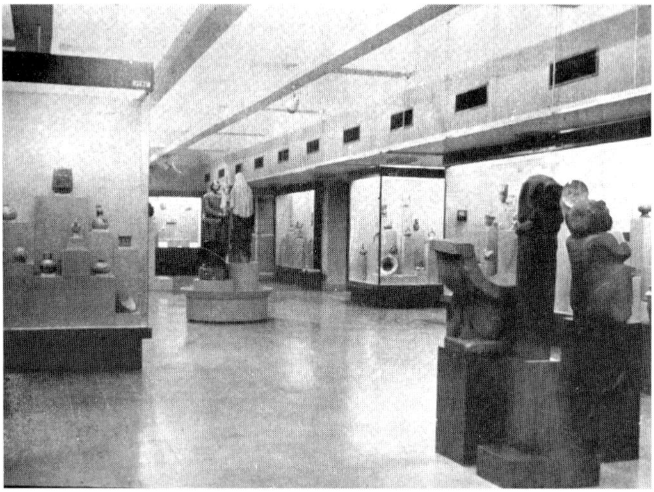

fig. 19. A general view of the Pre-Columbian Gallery, National Museum, New Delhi

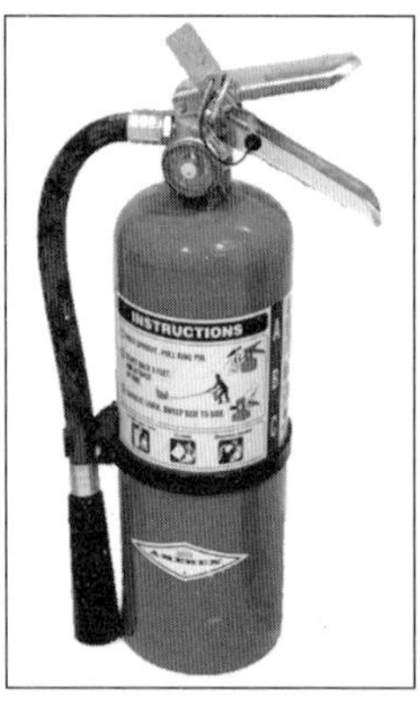

fig. 20. Fire Extinguisher.

Bibliography

Adams, Gene, 1989, *Museums and Galleries: A Teachers Handbook*, London: Hutchinson Education.

Agrawal, O.P., 1972, *Conservation in the Tropics*, Rome: International Centre for Conservation.

———, 1973, *Documentation in Museums*, New Delhi: Museums Association of India.

———, 1977, *Care and Preservation of Museum Objects*, New Delhi: NRLC.

———, 1979, *Security in Museums*, New Delhi: Museums Association of India.

———, 1984, *Conservation of Manuscripts and Paintings of South-East Asia*, London: Butterworths.

———, 1987, *Conservation of Metal in Humid Climate*, Proceedings of the Asian Regional Seminar held from 7-12 December 1987, New Delhi: NRLC.

———, 1992, *Conservation of Manuscript and Document*, Lucknow: INTACH.

———, 1993, *Preservation of Art Objects and Library Materials*, New Delhi: National Book Trust.

Agrawal, O.P. and Mandana Barkeshali, 2001, *Pustako Pandulipio tatha Kagazi Pralakho ka Sanrakshan*, New Delhi: Sandeep Prakashan.

Agrawal, O.P. and S.N. Sinha, 1992, *Conservation Status of Manuscripts, Books, Archival and Alike Material*, Lucknow: INTACH Conservation Institute.

Alexander, Edward P., 1995, *Museum Masters: Their Museums and Their Influences*, London: Altamira Press.

Ambrose, Timothy, 1987, *Education in Museums, Museums in Education*, Edinburgh: Scotttish Museum Council.

Ambrose, Timothy and Sue Runyard, 1991, *Forward Planning: A Handbook of Business, Corporate and Development Planning for Museums and Galleries*, London: Routledge.

Banerjee, N.R., 1990, *Museum and Cultural Heritage of India*, New Delhi: Agam Kala Prakashan.

Banerjee, Swapna, 2006, *Glimpses of Museums: The West Bengal Scenario*, Kolkata: Punthi Pustak.

Baxi, Smita J. and V.P. Dwivedi, 1973, *Modern Museum: Organization and Practice in India*, New Delhi: Abhinav Publication.

Behera, Bijay Kumar and Subodh Kumar Mohanty, 2007, *Museology and Museum Management*, Bhubaneshwar: Mayur Publications.

Belcher, Michael, 1991, *Exhibitions in Museums*, Washington DC: Smithsonian Institution Press.

Black, Graham, 2005, *The Engaging Museum: Developing Museums for Visitor Involvement*, London: Routledge.

Boswell, David and Jessica Evans, 1999, *Representing the Nation: A Reader Histories, Heritage and Museums*, New York: Routledge.

Boylan, Patrick, 1992, *Museums 2000*, London: Routledge.

Brawne, Michael, 1965, *The New Museum: Architecture and Display*, New York: Praegar Publishers.

Butler, Stella V.F., *Science and Technology Museums*, London: Leicester University Press.

Carbonell, Bettina Messias, 2004, *Museum Studies: An Anthology of Contexts*, UK: Blackwell Publishing.

Casser, May, 1995, *Environmental Management: Guidelines for Museums and Galleries*, London: Routledge.

Chakravarti, Shyamalkanti, 2004, *The Indian Museum 1814-1914*, Kolkata: Baptist Mission Press.

Chakravarty, K.K. and K.V. Sundaram, 2003, *Restoring Human Culture and Biospheric Environment: A New Museum Movement*, New Delhi: Northern Book Centre.

Chhabra, B.Ch., 1961, *Museums and Democracy*, Baroda: Department of Museology.

Choudhury, R.D., 1998, *Museums of India and Their Melodies*, New Delhi: Agam Kala Prakashan.

Corsane, Gerard, 2005, *Heritage, Museums and Galleries: An Introductory Reader*, London: Routledge.

Crane, Suresh A., 2000, *Museums and Memory*, Stanford: Stanford University Press.

Daifuku, Hiroshi, 1983, *The Conservation of Wooden Cultural Property*, Japan: National Research Institute of Cultural Property.

Danilow, Victor J., 1994, *Museum Careers and Training: A Professional Guide*, London: Greenwood Press.

Darragh, John and James S. Snyder, 1993, *Museum Design: Planning and Building of Art*, Oxford: Oxford University Press.

Davis, Peter, 1999, *Ecomuseums: A Sense of Peace*, London: Leicester University Press.

Dilevko, Juris and Lisa Gottlieb, 2004, *The Evolution of Library and Museum Partnerships*, London: Libraries Unlimited.

Donzel, Catherine, 1998, *New Museums*, Paris: Telleri.

Dwivedi, V.P. and G.N. Pant, 1980, *Museums and Museology: New Horizons*, New Delhi: Agam Kala Prakashan.

Edson, Gary, 1995, *International Directory of Museum Training*, London: Routledge.

———, 1997, *Museum Ethics*, London: Routledge.

Edson, Gary and David Dean, 1994, *The Handbook for Museums*, London: Routledge.

Finlay, Ian, 1977, *Priceless Heritage: The Future of Museums*, London: Faber and Faber Ltd.

Fladmark, J.M., 2000, *Heritage and Museum: Shaping National Identity*, Oxford: Alden Press.

Flower, William Henry, 1996, *Essays on Museums*, London: Routledge.

Ganeshan, R., 2002, *Bhartiya Sangrahalaya evam Jansamparka*, Varanasi: Vishvavidyala Prakashan.

Ghoshmaulik, S.K., 2001, *Understanding Heritage: Role of Museum*, Bhubaneswar: Utkal University.

Giebelhausen, Michaela, 2003, *The Architecture of the Museum: Symbolic Structures, Urban Contexts*, Manchester: Manchester University Press.

Glaser, Jane R. and Artemis A. Zenetou, 1994, *Gender Perspectives: Essays on Women in Museums*, Washington: Smithsonian Institution Press.

———, 1996, *Museums: A Place to Work : Planning Museum Careers*, London: Routledge.

Goel, Anil, 1998, *Museums and Collections of Delhi*, New Delhi: Harman Publishing House.

Goodlad, Sinclair and Stephanie Mcivor, 1998, *Museum Volunteers*, London: Routledge.

Gorman, G.E. and Sydney J. Shep, 2006, *Preservation Management for Libraries, Archives and Museums*, Cornwall: Facet Publishing.

Gupta, K.K., 1995, *Conservation of Cultural Property in India*, New Delhi: National Museum Institute.

———, 2006, *Restoration of Indian Miniature Paintings*, New Delhi: National Museum Institute.

Gupta, S.P., 1985, *Masterpieces from the National Museum Collection*, New Delhi: National Museum.

Gurian, Elaine Heumann, 2006, *Civilizing the Museum*, London: Routledge.

Hak, Abdul and Rene Bahler, 1970, *Field Manual for Museums*, Paris: UNESCO.

Hall, Patricia and Charlie Seemann, 1987, *Folklife and Museums: Selected Readings*, Tennessee: The American Association for State and Local Histry.

Harinarayana, N. and V. Jeyaraj, 1995, *Care of Museum Objects*, Madras: Government Museum.

Haxthausen, Charles W., 2002, *The Two Art Histories: The Museum and the Stories*, London: Yale University Press.

Hooper-Greenhill, Eilean, 1992, *Museums and the Shaping of Knowledge*, London: Routledge.

———, 1994, *The Educational Role of the Museum*, London: Routledge.

———, 1994, *Museums and Their Visitors*, London: Routledge.

———, 1997, *Cultural Diversity: Developing Museum Audiences in Britain*, London: Leicester University Press.

———, 2000, *Museums and the Interpretation of Visual Culture*, London: Routledge.

Hourston, Laura, 2004, *Museum Builders*, London: Wiley Academy.

Hudson, Kenneth, 1977, *Museums for the 1980s: A Survey of World Trends*, Paris: UNESCO.

Husain, Ahrar, 2001, *Museums of Delhi: Learning Resource Centers*, Delhi: Sana Publishers.

Jain, Sanjay, 2001, *Museums evam Museology: Ek Parichaya*, Baroda: Kanika Prakashan.

Jameson, John H. and Sherene Baugher, 2007, *Past Meets Present: Archaeologists Partnering with Museum Curators, Teachers and Community Groups*, New York: Springer.

John, M.A., 1984, *Manual of Curatorship*, London: Butterworths.

Journal of Indian Museums, vol. LI, 1994-95, New Delhi : Museums Association of India.

Kamalakar, G. and V. Pandit Rao, 1995, *Conservation, Preservation & Restoration: Tradition, Trends and Techniques*, Hyderabad: Birla Archaeological and Cultural Research Institute.

Kaplan, E.S., *Museums and the Making of Ourselves: The Role of Objects in National Identity*, London: Leicester University Press.

Karp, Ivan, 1992, *Museums and Communities: The Politics of Public Culture*, Washington: Smithsonian Institution Press.

———, 2006, *Museum Frictions*, London: Duke University Press.

Kavanagh, Gaynor, 1991, *The Museum Profession: Internal and External Relations*, Leicester: Leicester University Press.

———, 1994, *Museum Provision and Professionalism*, London: Routledge.

———, 1996, *Making Histories in Museums*, London: Leicester University Press.

Kavanagh, Gaynor and Elizabeth Frostick, 1998, *Making City Histories in Museums*, London: Leicester University Press.

Kirpal, P.N., *Problems and Trends in Museology*, New Delhi: Ministry of Education.

Lahkar, G.C., 1977, *A Short Note on Museology*, Assam: Sumitra Prakashan.

Lal, B.B. and S.P. Singh, 2007, *Ajanta Paintings: Their Composition, Technique, Deterioration and Presentation*, New Delhi: Islamic Wonders Bureau.

Lamugnani, Vittorio Magnago and Angel Sachs, *Museums for New Milllennium: Concepts Projects Buildings*, Munich: Prestel.

Layfon, Robert, Peter G. Stone and Julian Thomas, 2001, *Destruction and Conservation of Cultural Property*, London: Routledge.

Light, R.B. and D.A. Roberts, 1986, *Museum Documentation System: Development and Applications*, London: Butterworths.

Liston, David, 1993, *Museum Security and Protection*, London: Routledge.

Lord, Gail Dexter and Barry Lord, 1999, *The Manual of Museum Planning*, London: The Stationary Office.

Lumley, Robert, 1988, *The Museum Time Machine*, London: Routledge.

Macdonald, Sharon, 2006, *A Companion to Museum Studies*, USA: Blackwell Publishing.

Maleuvre, Didier, 1999, *Museum Memories: History, Technology, Art*, Stanford: Stanford University Press.

Marshell, John, 1923, *Conservation Manual*, Delhi: Caxton Publications.

Matthews, Geoff, 1991, *Museum and Art Galleries: Design and Development Guides*, Oxford: Butterworth Architecture.

Merriman, Nick, 1999, *Making Early Histories in Museums*, Leicester: Leicester University Press.

Moore, Kevin, 1997, *Museum Management*, London: Routledge.

Museums Without Barriers: A New Deal for Disabled People, Foundation De France and ICOM, 1991, London: Routledge.

Newson, Barbara Y. and Adele Z. Silver, *The Art Museum as Educator*, Berkeley: University of California Press.

Nigam, M.L., 1966, *Fundamentals of Museology*, Hyderabad: Navahind Prakashan.

Olofsson, Ulla Keding, 1979, *Museums and Children*, Paris: UNESCO.

Paine, Crispin, 2000, *Godly Things: Museums, Objects and Religion*, London: Leicester University Press.

Pearce, Susan M., 1989, *Museum Studies in Material Culture*, Leicester: Leicester University Press.

———, 1990, *Archaeological Curatorship*, London: Leicester University Press.

———, 1992, *Museums Objects and Collections: A Cultural Study*, Leicester: Leicester University Press.

———, 1994, *Interpreting Objects and Collections*, London: Routledge.

Peers, Laura and Alison K. Brown, *Museums and Source Communities: A Routledge Reader*, London: Routledge.

Pegler, Martin M., 2001, *Contemporary Exhibit Design*, New York: Visual Reference Publications.

Pollock, Griselda and Zemans Joyce, 2007, *Museums after Modernism: Strategies for Engagement*, USA: Blackwell Publishing.

Punja, Shobita, 1990, *Museums of India*, Hong Kong: The Guidebook Company Ltd.

Report of the Central Museums Review Committee, 1972, New Delhi: Ministry of Education, GOI.

Roy, D.K., 2006, *Some Cute Points*, Delhi: Kalpaz Publications.

Sandell, Richard, 2007, *Museums, Prejudice and the Reframing of Difference*, London: Routledge.

Sarkar, H., 1981, *Museums and Protection of Monuments and Antiquities in India*, Delhi: Sandeep Prakashan.

Schroeder-Gudehus, Brigitte, 2003, *Industrial Society & its Museums*, Switzerland: Harwood Academic Publishers.

Sehgal, Narendra K., 2005, *The Changing Role of Science Centres and Museums in Developing Countries*, New Delhi: Daya Publishing House.

Shapiro, Michael Steven and Louis Ward Kemp, 1990, *The Museum: A Reference Guide*, New York: Greenwood Press.

Sherman, Daniel J. and Irit Rogoff, 1994, *Museum Culture*, London: Routledge.

Simpson, Moira G., 1996, *Making Representations: Museums in the Post Colonial Era*, London: Routledge.

Singh, A.P., 1987, *Conservation of Museum Techniques*, Delhi: Agam Kala Prakashan.

Sivaramamuti, C., 1959, *Directory of Museums in India*, New Delhi: Ministry of Scientific Research & Cultural Affairs.

Stephens, Suzanne, 1986, *Building the New Museum*, New York: The Archaeological League of New York.

Stone, Peter G. and Brian L. Molyneaux, 1994, *The Presented Past: Heritage, Museums and Education*, London: Routledge.

Talboys, Graeme K., 2000, *Museum Educator's Handbook*, England: Gower Publishing Ltd.

Vinas, Salvador Munor, 2005, *Contemporary Theory of Conservation*, Amsterdam: Elsevier.

Watson, Sheila, 2007, *Museums and Their Communities*, London: Routledge.

Weil, Stephen E., 1990, *Rethinking the Museum and Other Meditations*, Washington: Smithsonian Institution Press.

———, 2002, *Making Museum Matter*, Washington: Smithsonian Institution Press.

White, Anne, 1968, *Visiting Museums*, London: Faber & Faber.

Witcomb, Andrea, 2003, *Re-Imagining the Museum Beyond the Mausoleum*, London: Routledge.

Wittlin, Alma S., 1970, *Museums in Search of Usable Future*, Cambridge: The MIT Press.

Woodhead, Peter and Geoffrey Stansfield, 1994, *Museum Studies*, London: Mansell Publishing Ltd.

Index